KT-526-260

Making Dyslexia Work for You

A SELF-HELP GUIDE

Vicki Goodwin and Bonita Thomson

CRAVEN COLLEGE

 David Fulton Publishers

David Fulton Publishers Ltd
The Chiswick Centre, 414 Chiswick High Road, London W4 5TF

www.fultonpublishers.co.uk

First published in Great Britain in 2004 by David Fulton Publishers

10 9 8 7 6 5 4 3 2

Note: The rights of Vicki Goodwin and Bonita Thomson to be identified as the
authors of this work have been asserted by them in accordance with the
Copyright, Designs and Patents Act 1988.

David Fulton Publishers is a division of Granada Learning Limited, part of ITV plc.

Copyright © Vicki Goodwin and Bonita Thomson 2004

British Library Cataloguing in Publication Data
A catalogue record for this book is available from the British Library.

ISBN 1-84312-091-7

Pages from this book may be photocopied for use only in the purchasing
institution. Otherwise, all rights reserved. No part of this publication may be
reproduced, stored in a retrieval system or transmitted, in any form or by any
means, electronic, mechanical, photocopying, or otherwise, without the prior
permission of the publishers.

Typeset by Mark Heslington, Northallerton, North Yorkshire
Printed and bound in Great Britain

AB
H 19383

371.914

MAKING DYSLEXIA WORK FOR YOU

**This book is to be returned on or before
the last date stamped below.**

PLEASE CHECK
FOR CD-ROM
ON ISSUE AND
RETURN

- 3 OCT 2006
- 4 JAN 2007
- 3 JUL 2009

1 JUN 2010

0 JAN
15 NOV 2012
- 3 MAY 2019

06.06.24
WITHDRAWN
CRAVEN COLLEGE
SJS

LIBREX

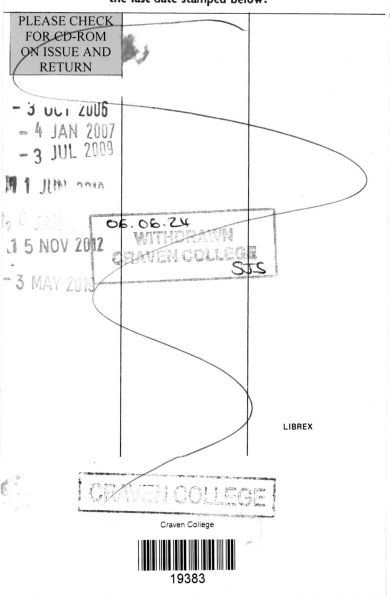

CRAVEN COLLEGE

Craven College

19383

£10-74

Contents

Acknowledgements

We would like to acknowledge all the wisdom and experience that so many dyslexic adults have generously shared with us.

We would like to thank the many colleagues from whom we have learnt so much over the years.

Our thanks also go to our long-suffering partners for their patience and encouragement.

Some of the activities, strategies and illustrations in this book first appeared in the Dyslexia Toolkit (Goodwin & Thomson 1999), funded and published by the Open University.

Vicki Goodwin wishes to thank the Open University for allowing her time to read and research for this book.

We are indebted to Ian Rowney for technical advice and his work in putting together the CD-ROM, and to Jenny Lee for allowing us to include her spelling programme, MUSP, adapted for using without a tutor.

Introduction

When we first thought about writing a book for dyslexic adults we seriously wondered if we were doing the right thing. Would someone with dyslexia want to *read* our book if we could present it in an accessible way? We think you will.

Not everyone gets help when they need it. This is a book to help you. You can dip into it and come back to it as often as you need. We hope it will stimulate you to try some of the ideas and create more of your own. We really want you to discover things for yourself because these are the things that usually work best; many of the ideas and strategies included have been devised by dyslexic adults.

If you know very little about dyslexia, then start at the beginning. Part 1 covers some of the things we now know about the dyslexic brain and the range of associated difficulties and strengths.

Part 2 is your 'toolbox'. If you don't know what you are looking for, you can move through the headings until you find what interests you. It introduces a variety of strategies for you to build on and develop for specific situations:

- the world of print
- written communications
- planning and organisation
- numbers and memory

Part 3 is about resources and how information technology (IT) can help. It also explores some wider issues about dyslexia in daily life, especially education and the workplace.

We hope that your family, friends, tutors and employers will also find the book useful.

The enclosed CD-ROM

We have included a CD-ROM on which you will find all the printable documents used in the book, and also lots of other useful information which you can dip into whenever you want to find out more about many of the topics raised. The entire text of the book is also included on the CD-ROM. If your screen-reader can work with Adobe pdf files, you will be able to listen to the text as you read it.

If you do not have access to a computer that can read it, your local library or an internet café can help. Please ask permission to use the CD-ROM from whoever is running that location, and tell them that running the CD-ROM does not involve writing any files to their computers.

If the CD-ROM doesn't start up automatically, you can start it by double-clicking on the file named 'index.htm'. You will be able to find this by opening up Windows Explorer and clicking the link to the CD-ROM or DVD drive in which you have placed this disk. It will usually be the 'D', sometimes the 'E' drive.

Part 1
Dyslexia and You

There are three chapters in Part 1.

Chapter 1: Exploring your dyslexia
What dyslexia is, and feelings about being dyslexic

Chapter 2: Finding out about dyslexia
What we know about dyslexia and the brain

Chapter 3: Finding out about the way you learn and what you need
Finding out about your dyslexia and your needs

Although you don't *need* to read Part 1 first, you will find something here to get you thinking about how dyslexia affects you. We help you to understand what is happening in your brain and identify your strengths. Armed with this knowledge you can move confidently on to Part 2.

1

Exploring your dyslexia

If you understand where you are you can at least aim for where you want to go.

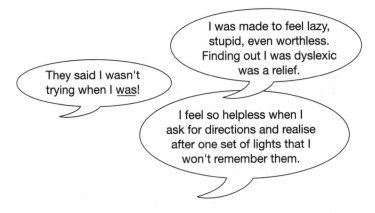

I was made to feel lazy, stupid, even worthless. Finding out I was dyslexic was a relief.

They said I wasn't trying when I <u>was</u>!

I feel so helpless when I ask for directions and realise after one set of lights that I won't remember them.

How does it feel to be dyslexic?

Some of the descriptions of how it feels to be dyslexic are about feelings of frustration. Simple things such as reading and writing can seem oddly difficult. Words simply won't go where you want them. Organisation can be an issue too. Losing your way, trying to read aloud, struggling to keep up with work – all contribute to a general sense of exhaustion and lack of confidence. This is about living in a world where most people are *not* dyslexic.

There can also be a feeling of enormous energy when everything seems to come together and you realise you have understood a situation or problem in a wholly unique and remarkable way. Tom West, in his book, *In the Mind's Eye* (see appendix B), shows that many dyslexic thinkers have an unusual balance of skills which are often outstandingly creative.

✍ ACTIVITY 1 – How does it feel for you?

Take a moment to think about how your dyslexia affects you. Think about these questions – tick the answers that are closest to yours.

• What do you find most frustrating?	Reading so slowly. Not being able to get down on paper what I want to say. Forgetting words or names. Having illegible or uneven handwriting. Misreading words. Not being able to spell words. Not being able to find something. Being late.
• How do you think others see you?	Lazy. Creative. Disorganised. Untidy. Quirky. Intuitive. Inspired. Determined. Slow. Other – what?
• What are your particular strengths?	Generating ideas. Thinking holistically. Solving problems. Being artistic. Being musical. Having empathy. Getting things done. Inspiring others. Visual-spatial awareness.

Do *you* think you are dyslexic?

You may be looking through this book because you have recently had an assessment which suggests you are dyslexic. You may have had an assessment as a child. If you are reading this because you are still wondering whether you are dyslexic, look at the initial screening checklist (appendix A) and read at least the last part of this chapter. You can print a copy of the checklist from the CD-ROM 5, printable documents.

Effects of dyslexia

Almost everyone will experience some difficulties in everyday life, but people with dyslexia will encounter many such as:

- Reading, which is likely to be slow.
- Concentration, which tends to fluctuate.

- Spelling and grammar, which can be unorthodox.
- Physical coordination and handwriting.
- Remembering information.
- Organising and planning.
- Working within time limits.
- Thinking and working in sequences.
- Visual difficulties such as blurring and distortion of print.
- Good and bad days.

All these can make a difficult situation worse – or even impossible on a bad day. Inexplicably things just don't seem to fit together in your head; you cannot make the connections. You can't seem to work properly at anything on one day and you can on another.

How do people find out if they are dyslexic?

There are many ways in which people discover their dyslexia. Usually it doesn't come as a total surprise; it confirms something they have suspected for some time.

> *Suddenly I realised all these different difficulties were all connected. It felt like the final pieces in a jigsaw had fallen into place. It explained so much.*

The subject of dyslexia may come up in a number of different ways:

Your teacher may suggest that you are dyslexic.
A member of your family or someone else may suggest the possibility that you have dyslexia.
One of your children may be assessed as being dyslexic.
A news item may describe dyslexia in a way that rings bells for you.
At college or in the workplace someone may suggest dyslexia as being the cause of difficulties you are experiencing.

A combination of some of these may gradually raise your awareness of dyslexia and you may decide to find out more. Let's look more closely at these through personal experiences.

At school: primary school
In a primary school setting a teacher might notice that a child seems to be making inconsistent progress. An otherwise outgoing child may be slow in learning to read and curiously reluctant to read out loud. They may produce unusual spellings but appear highly articulate and able to grasp concepts quickly. Sometimes, at this stage, a child might be screened for dyslexia and given some additional teaching. In primary

education a class tends to have the same teacher for all subjects so it is easier to be aware of the child who is having difficulties. But it is possible for difficulties of a very bright child or a quiet child to go unnoticed as long as their progress is average.

Here is one person's story:

When I went to school I was very excited about the prospect of learning to read and write. I loved stories and books. I didn't realise for a while that I was having a hard time trying to make sense of the letters and words until we began to read aloud and to read words that weren't in my reading book – I knew those off by heart.

When I started writing stories I had so much to say but the teacher marked almost every word wrong and told me I had to do something about my spelling. I felt crushed. My exciting story packed full of ideas didn't seem to count for anything.

Every day there was something I had forgotten or lost. One day it was my reading book and a note for the teacher, another day my pencil case and bus pass.

I still hadn't managed to read properly by the time I was nine and dreaded reading lessons because I was so slow compared with all the others in the class. Writing was even worse – I never seemed to complete anything. I can remember a lot of red crosses and the critical comments on the bottom: 'You must make more effort'. As if I wasn't!

At school: secondary school
In the secondary school situation there is usually a different teacher for most subjects; this makes it much more difficult to spot individual inconsistencies. Difficulties may not be noticed or may be regarded as 'laziness' or lack of ability. If they are picked up, then the young person may get an assessment and some structured support. However, a number of people get through the school system without having dyslexia identified – they may get by on their natural ability or wit, or they may be wrongly identified as slow learners or disruptive pupils. For them a proper assessment comes very late. As a result, they may not have been taught learning methods and study skills that suit them. Despite putting in tremendous effort they will have little to show for it. Learning seems to be so difficult, giving rise to considerable frustration and feelings of inadequacy. It is not surprising that many are 'turned off' school and learning.

Another dyslexic adult remembers:

> It was only in class discussions that I found I was able to explain what I wanted to say and they realised I had in fact understood a lot of what was being taught. I could listen and understand, but I couldn't write it down. I would get stuck on one unfamiliar word and then lose the thread of the sentence. I could write the homework down slowly or get to the next class on time. By playing the clown I managed to avoid some of the scorn. I pretended that it was because I was scatty that I forgot, was late, missed the homework etc. That was more acceptable a label than 'lazy' or 'stupid'.

Pause

Does any of what you have read so far chime for you? You might like to highlight some of the words and phrases in the experiences above that ring particularly loud bells.

Family or other people

Often a parent is concerned as to why their son or daughter is struggling at school. They are not put off by teachers' comments such as 'let's see how they go' year after year. They start finding out a bit more about dyslexia.

> As a parent I remember looking at my son's history test when he was about nine. The teacher had marked every single answer as wrong and put 0/10 at the bottom but when I looked through the test I recognised that he had got more than half the answers right. He had misspelled 'battle' as 'battel' and 'conqueror' became 'conqerer'. Every answer had a spelling mistake. I decided to investigate.

A parent's enquiries may either lead to an investigation by the school, or they themselves may decide to learn more about dyslexia to find ways to help the child directly. If an older brother or sister had similar problems then a parent may be quicker in suspecting that there is a similar difficulty. It is also possible that, at this stage, some parents may begin to question whether their own difficulties could be due to dyslexia.

Comments about dyslexia from other people in general conversation may have led you to think about difficulties you may have that are similar.

> I wonder if I could be dyslexic – you know. I find that difficult too.

From a news item
Features and news items about dyslexia crop up frequently in the media, for example, a scientific report:

STUDY FINDS GENE LINKED TO DYSLEXIA
The first gene to be linked to the learning disorder dyslexia has been identified ... The discovery could lead to a better understanding of the disability and ways to overcome it ... not everyone with the mutation would develop the disorder.

or a new theory about how best to teach literacy:

THE READING BRAIN
Researchers use brain scans to investigate changes in the brain activity of dyslexic children as they use the reading programme ...

An article may report on an achievement by someone with dyslexia or a new piece of technology that could be useful. Most features include at least one account of someone's experience of struggling with print or failing at school, which may strike a chord and send you scurrying off for more information.

I saw this article about people who found the print was constantly moving on the page and I recognised the description immediately. It was me!

At college or in the workplace
In further or higher education, about half the students who have dyslexic-type difficulties are either unaware of their dyslexia or do not mention it when they go into further or higher education. If they are lucky a tutor may spot that they are having difficulties with written work and encourage them to seek advice.

It was OK at school. I just didn't take notes. I sometimes borrowed other people's and photocopied them. I mainly just read and reread as much as I could of the text books we were given. When I got to college there was just too much reading to be able to do that and I started falling behind.

In the workplace, people sometimes discover that they may be dyslexic or have it confirmed when their job changes. They may have been promoted because they were good at their job and showed promise. They then find that their new job requires more literacy skills. Their boss or line manager knows they work hard and, surprised at their difficulties, they may suspect dyslexia. Staff in human resource (personnel) departments are usually quite knowledgeable about a range of disabilities and difficulties these days – they have to be because of the Disability Discrimination Act 1995. They may suggest a work evaluation and a diagnostic assessment.

I suppose I had deliberately chosen work that allowed me to avoid too much reading and writing but actually I loved jewellery design and became very successful. The problems came when the company expanded and I was asked to take on some training that involved written materials. Then I panicked.

'It all seemed to add up'

Some dyslexic people have a very clear sense of the different way they respond to print, how they can never remember some words, how they feel confused by the letters. Some feel frustrated because they can't see their spelling mistakes. Others have vivid recollections of getting lost, trying to follow directions or instructions but always arriving late no matter how hard they try. A non-dyslexic person may sympathise with such experiences and may experience them occasionally too. But there is almost a deep sigh of recognition from dyslexic people: it all seems to add up.

This personal account illustrates the sense of frustration an able person can feel:

He started explaining how I needed to copy what I was writing onto a floppy disk. This had to be a copy of what was on my hard disk. Between the dragging of the pointer and the right or left clicking and holding and copying and saving and icons and the different names of folders and documents, I felt more and more tearful and confused. How could I know what was in which folder or document? If I couldn't see them – how did I know they existed? Hopelessly, the tears of frustration streaked down my face as I tried to wrestle my thoughts into the garble of words. 'You just have to copy this to . . . Whenever you write this just go into . . .' The words ebbed and flowed ceaselessly. Unless I pretended to agree, to nod wisely, to indicate that I followed what he said – he would go on trying so hard to explain things carefully and simply. I could just about follow the words, but each time he rephrased things to help me understand, it felt like another set of information to grapple with. I knew with a sinking feeling that I could not remember any of it beyond the sound of his last word.

Four stories

Yasmin, aged 8

Yasmin's mother suspected she was having more than usual problems with learning to read. Her elder sister had been assessed for dyslexia when she was nine and so Yasmin's mum queried her progress a little earlier. It took over two years before any extra support was given and a further year for an assessment to be carried out. By the time Yasmin went to secondary school she had begun to make some progress and was more confident in herself.

Bill, aged 16

Bill had experienced a lot of difficulty at school from the start of his secondary years. The work that had been more gently criticised before was now being sent back, and the larger school with its corridors and different places made it all even more confusing. To save face, Bill began to misbehave – better to be thought of as awkward rather than slow – especially with his peers. In his GCSE year, one of his teachers suggested that he should be screened for dyslexia and this led to him being assessed. He got some extra help after school and began to make progress, especially in the subjects he liked. He found the use of a computer made a big difference in the work he could do and decided to go on into the sixth form. With extra time in examinations he was able to get into university although he still avoided too much reading.

Charles, aged 30

Charles didn't discover his dyslexia for many years. Living and working on a farm in the former Rhodesia he was considered 'slow'. When he had to enlist in the army he was discharged after an initial training period because he was unable to march in time. He came to the UK and worked for a long time in residential care homes until he was encouraged to get qualifications in social care. It was only then he came for assessment and was helped in his part-time studies, managing to pass several courses.

Mary, aged 48

Mary had muddled through school never doing particularly well. Her talent in art and design led her to art college and she developed a career in fabric design. After several successful years her firm wanted to promote her and urged her to take a qualification in business administration to help her in her new senior position. She began to panic, realising that she found writing and organising materials very difficult. She sought study skills advice and it was then suggested that she might have dyslexia. Following her assessment she was offered help planning her studies and managed to complete the qualification.

Your own story

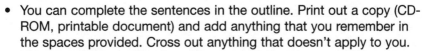 **ACTIVITY 2** – Writing your own story

Now we would like you to write your own story. This will help you to bring together all your feelings and experiences which may relate to your dyslexia. You can choose how you would like to do it:

- You can complete the sentences in the outline. Print out a copy (CD-ROM, printable document) and add anything that you remember in the spaces provided. Cross out anything that doesn't apply to you.
- You can use the outline to guide you and complete your story on a separate sheet.
- You can just let it flow onto paper in any order – forget spelling etc.
- You could speak it onto tape.

My Story

This is an outline for you to add the details. Complete any sentences to give more information about you. Add anything that you remember in the spaces provided. Cross out anything that doesn't apply to you.

Before I went to school
I was slow learning to talk. I had difficulty pronouncing words ...
I was generally healthy ...
I had some hearing problems ...
I had some visual problems ...
I was clumsy. I had difficulties with tying shoelaces, ball games ...

My family
The language(s) spoken at home was (were) ....
Other people in my family had difficulty with reading, spelling, writing, coordination, including my ....
Of these my ....
had a diagnosis of dyslexia.

At primary school
I remember being late learning to read. The words and letters ...
I hated reading aloud ...
I found writing difficult because ...
I was left/right-handed ...
I had difficulty remembering the times tables ...
The attitude of my teachers to my difficulties was ...

I had extra help for ...
I enjoyed primary school. I particularly liked ...

At secondary school
My difficulties increased. In particular I found ...
Languages were difficult for me. I tried to learn .... but ...
I felt I worked hard/I think I was rather lazy/I used to bunk off school.
My teachers were ...
I passed ... O-levels/CSEs/GCSEs in ...
I passed ... A-levels/Btec in ...
I left school aged ...
After school I did some more studying ...

At work
I started working in ...
I enjoyed my work/I hated my work.
I now work as ...
The attitude of my boss and/or colleagues to my difficulties is ...
I think I could progress further in my job if ...

Me
The things I really find difficult include ...
I try to avoid ...
I have some good ways of getting round things such as ...
Things that I am good at include ...
I really enjoy ...
My most important aim in life is to ...

Compare your story with those in the text above. Do you notice some things that are the same? You might have some unanswered questions. Be aware that dyslexia can overlap with other specific learning difficulties.

Other specific learning difficulties (SpLD)

There are a range of specific learning difficulties, some of which are closely related to dyslexia. Although there is not space here to discuss these in detail, we have included a summary of the terms you may come across. The symptoms of all the SpLDs may overlap, i.e. you may be dyslexic with some dyspraxic difficulties or you may have attention deficit hyperactive disorder (ADHD) with some dyslexic-type difficulties. Although these are just labels, they can sometimes be helpful (e.g. for getting particular support). However, they may sometimes be unhelpful – use them only as you need or want to.

Dyspraxia: literally means 'difficulty with doing'. It is an impairment of the brain cells responsible for the organisation of movement. This affects the planning of what to do and how to do it.

Dyscalculia: means 'difficulty performing mathematical calculations'. This does not apply to the grasping of mathematical concepts.

Attention Deficit Disorder (ADD): a medical condition that affects the ability to concentrate and maintain attention to tasks.

Attention Deficit Hyperactive Disorder (ADHD): inattention combined with significantly heightened activity levels and impulsiveness.

Just be aware that a specific learning difficulty is independent of general ability (intelligence) but can seriously get in the way of someone managing to do something that they would be expected to be capable of doing. It is therefore frustrating for that person as they have to devise or be helped to find ways round the problem which will involve a lot of effort and time.

Taking time to assess yourself

There are many dyslexia checklists available. We have included one (appendix a/CD-ROM ⊘) but you may have already been through a list supplied by the British Dyslexia Association (BDA) or the Adult Dyslexia Organisation (ADO). There are lots of checklists on the Internet too. All these checklists are designed to help you decide whether you might be dyslexic.

If you are reading this book because you think you might be dyslexic, now is the time to go through the checklist, add up the ticks and then think about what to do next. Here are a couple of options:

- find a qualified assessor and discuss with him/her whether you need a full assessment (chapter 3 looks at what this involves);
- accept that you may be dyslexic and use this book for ideas to help you do those tasks with which you have the most difficulty.

There is no doubt that for some people the identification or diagnosis of dyslexia comes as a blessing. It is a relief to know you are not 'malingering' and that some of the comments you may have received in the past were indeed totally unfair.

It came as a huge relief to me – at last I knew I wasn't a fraud! I hadn't just been lazy. Trying any harder wouldn't have worked.

✍ ACTIVITY 3 – Identifying things to work on

Take a moment to think about situations that you find difficult.

- Jot down a few things you find difficult.
- Assess how difficult: hard, very hard, impossible.
- Rank each item in order of how important it is to you – with 1 being the most important.

You should end up with a list like this:

Things I find difficult	How difficult	How important
Spelling	Very	1
Remembering names	Virtually impossible	3
Coping with so much reading	Hard	2

Print out the blank document from the CD-ROM, printable documents to make your list. Stick your list on a piece of card the same size as this book and use it as a bookmark! It will be a useful reminder of your aims.

In this chapter we have looked at:

- how you might feel about dyslexia;
- how you found out about your dyslexia;
- how it affects you;
- what you'd like to work on to improve.

We hope we have encouraged you to think. Mull it all over before you read on. You don't have to progress by taking each chapter in order. If something has triggered your curiosity in another chapter, that's fine – do it your way.

2
Finding out about dyslexia

Understanding something about the science behind your dyslexia will help you to understand what might be going on in your brain.

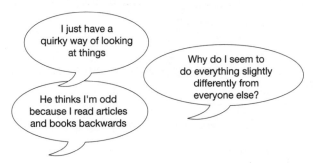

Do any of these ring a bell? You might like to add a comment about you.

Dyslexic brains are different. That's official. There is scientific evidence to show that the dyslexic brain processes information differently. For example, with various brain-scanning techniques we can now see what is happening in our brains when doing particular tasks; the scanner measures which bits of the brain are active. We know that dyslexic brains tend to be more active in the right side which is called the right hemisphere.

This chapter looks at some of the evidence and what it might mean for you.

How we read

Reading makes considerable demands on us that are quite different from speaking. We have to learn the rules:

- we have to know what sounds the letters represent;
- we have to know how to put the sounds together to make words.

Can you remember learning to read? Can you remember having any of the following difficulties?

 CRAVEN COLLEGE

	Tick here
Couldn't remember the different sounds of the vowels: a e i o u	
Couldn't tell the difference between some letters such as p and q, b and d	
Had difficulty with pronouncing th and f	
Couldn't remember the sounds for 'ough' in though, through, cough, enough, bough	

Circle any of these words that describe how you remember having felt at the time:

frustrated angry resigned foolish	
perplexed tired other?	

Reading involves two processes: processing sound information and processing visual information. You may not be familiar with the term 'phonology' (pronounced fo-nol-ogy). Briefly, phonology is the study of sounds that are found in language. This means the sounds used when you *speak*, not the sounds made when you scream, laugh or cough.

Put simply, the two things that the brain is doing are:

- linking the letters to sounds – phonology;
- matching the look of the word to what it has seen before – visual.

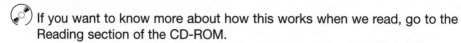 If you want to know more about how this works when we read, go to the Reading section of the CD-ROM.

There is a big difference in how dyslexic people cope with these two skills – they are usually much better at the visual analysis. The following diagram shows how the tasks are divided between different parts of the brain:

The Planning Centre
The front part of the brain:
for planning, sequencing,
change, new things and
attention

The Sound Centre
The left-hand side of the brain:
where sounds are processed –
letters are linked to sounds and
sounds to letters

The Visual-Spatial Centre
The right-hand side of the brain:
where visual information is
processed and awareness of
space is handled

Figure 1 Adapted from the model of Alan Baddeley (*Working Memory,* Oxford: Clarendon Press, 1986)

We have oversimplified the real situation. If your phonological processing (the 'sound centre') is inefficient then your visual processing (the 'visual-spatial centre') will make up for it. However, the visual route is slower. It is also hopelessly unreliable for long words and totally useless for new words. You probably have difficulty reading words you've never encountered before. Look at the words on this list. You may not have met them before. Try reading them aloud:

> pathognomonic
> homunculus
> reafference
> diphenylbutyl

We can't check whether you've got them right but we suspect that you would struggle to read them straight off because they are probably unfamiliar to you.

You may also have experienced muddling words that look very similar. Try these pairs:

> beautify *and* beatify
> spilt *and* split
> affect *and* effect

You may not have spotted the difference between each word in the pair at first reading.

Look back at the diagram in Figure 1. When you are reading, the 'visual-spatial centre' may let you down. As you read through texts, your visual-spatial centre:

- can't recognise a word you've never met before;
- may mistake one word for another.

If your 'sound centre' works well, it will deal with these situations by recognising the letter sounds and putting them together. This is called 'phonological awareness'. But, in dyslexia, the processing in the 'sound centre' is often very inefficient so you have to rely more on the 'visual-spatial centre'. Reading becomes slower and harder.

In summary,

- Phonology is about the way that sounds relate to letters.
- You need phonological skills to read efficiently.
- In dyslexia, phonological skills (the sound centre processes) are usually underdeveloped.
- Dyslexics tend to rely on the slower, less reliable, visual-spatial centre.

The sound centre: phonology and phonological awareness
Your phonological skills should develop *before* you learn to read. There are three stages in the development of phonological skills. These are summarised in this table and explained below.

1. Awareness of syllables *You beat them out*	foot-ball-er (footballer)
2. Onset and rime *You learn tongue twisters and nursery rhymes*	b-ounce
3. Phoneme *You can hear the different sounds in a word*	sh-ee-p

Pause

With dyslexia, some or all of these skills are never fully developed.

Can you beat out syllables correctly?
Can you hear the difference in your head between the first sound of a word and the rest?
Can you count the number of sounds in each word?

 If you want to check these skills, go to the Reading section of the CD-ROM and click on *Check phonological skills*.

The visual-spatial centre: recognising words by sight

The right-hand side of the brain does most of the work when it comes to recognising words by sight. This is very useful for those short frequent words we need such as: the, and, a, it, no, not, etc. The brain can get quite good at recognising longer words too – particularly those that you use regularly. But the visual-spatial centre can get it wrong.

- It simply may not spot the difference as we demonstrated earlier with the pairs of words.
- Or it may think it's guessing the right word when it is, in fact, choosing a similar one: such as reading *identify* for *indemnify* thus getting the meaning of the sentence all wrong.
- If you are concentrating very hard on decoding the words, you may miss some of the little words such as 'not' for example. Missing 'not' changes the whole meaning completely.

Learning to read and write

The skills we need to learn to read and write are listed below. Often all these skills may not be present or well developed in dyslexic children. And the difficulties can persist into adulthood.

Skills required to learn to read and write	Examples
Knowing the letters of the alphabet and what they are called	Being able to distinguish b from d
Recognising syllables	Being able to beat out the number of syllables correctly
The linking of sounds to letters or groups of letters (phoneme knowledge)	Knowing the sound made by the letters 'ai', 'sch'. 'ing', 'bl'
Ability to take sounds away from a word and know what sounds are left	As with spoonerisms, e.g. chish and fips – see CD-ROM
Holding sounds and words in the short-term memory	Putting together the sounds to make words and words together to mean something

Skills required to learn to read and write	Examples
Ability to pronounce complex words	Coping with words such as anemone, specific, etc.
Knowing the meaning of a lot of words	Having a good hearing vocabulary
Being able to recognise word sounds from other sounds	Such as knowing that they are words rather than rubbish

Look at the visual representation of the skills we need; you can begin to see why some people have difficulties!

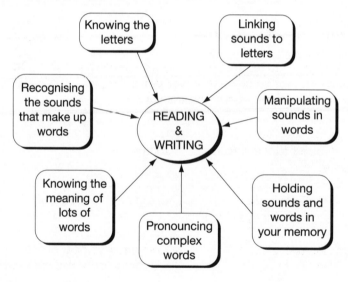

Figure 2

If some of these skills are absent or poorly developed, the result is that learning to read and write is exceptionally difficult. You may have vivid memories of what it felt like.

Reading is about *decoding* what's in front of you.

Writing is about *coding* what is in your head.

🕮 If you want to think a little more about these skills then go to the General section on the CD-ROM and click on *Reading & writing skills*.

The English language

The English language presents additional problems for dyslexic people compared with a language such as Italian for example. English is a 'non-transparent' language which means that:

- sounds are not always represented by the same letters

   a
   The 'long |a|' sound, as the word **bay**, can be written as in: mate,

   bait,

   and the word 'a' itself.

- letters and groups of letters do not always sound the same.

   ough
   Just look at how many ways 'ough' can be pronounced: bough, rough, through, thorough, cough!!!

So this huge variation has implications for reading, writing and spelling for us all. It is very bad news if you are dyslexic.

Italian, on the other hand, is an example of a 'transparent' language. The sound of a letter or group of letters never varies:

Que sera, sera!

So the English language is full of challenges. You will need, as always, to be creative with your learning. This is what Part 2 of this book is all about.

Inside the dyslexic brain

The dyslexic brain and how it functions is part of the branch of science called 'neuroscience'. There have been great strides forward in the last ten or so years in understanding how the brain functions generally.

The human brain has two parts called hemispheres, joined together near the middle. It is asymmetric: the right hemisphere is a bit smaller than the left. In the late 1980s post mortem work on the brains of dyslexic people showed that, compared to non-dyslexics, the dyslexic brain:

- is more symmetrical, i.e. the right side is significantly larger than in non-dyslexics;
- has a difference in structure including in the part that joins the two hemispheres.

During the 1990s great advances in scanning techniques allowed scientists to watch which parts of the brain are activated when doing certain tasks. Scanning is a non-invasive way of seeing how our internal organs, including the brain, are functioning.

As scientists gradually pieced together the evidence, it became clear that, in dyslexia:

- Left hemisphere language areas of the brain are less well developed.
- The areas of the brain involved in reading and writing do not work together as they should.
- The information flow between them is inefficient.
- Information gets jumbled up.
- Brains in those dyslexic adults who experience few difficulties now, still process information differently from non-dyslexics.
- The structure of the brain is different.
- Automatic tasks are affected – see information on *The cerebellum* on the CD-ROM ⊙.
- Fluency can be slow.

Input or output through:	Type of brain cell affected:	Effects:
The ears: auditory information	Auditory cells	Sound confusion and weak phonological awareness
The eyes: visual information	Visual cells	Visual confusion and distortion
Touch and general awareness in particular: movement information	Cells involved in controlling movement	Causes clumsiness and poor coordination

In the extreme, this means that words cannot be understood and articulated at the same time. This may explain, among other things, why it is so difficult to read out loud. Does it explain why you find some things difficult or impossible?

Many dyslexics experience visual difficulties that do not seem to be corrected with spectacles. Print on a page, particularly black on white, is uncomfortable to read. It can distort, swirl around, jump about and pulsate as illustrated in Figure 3.

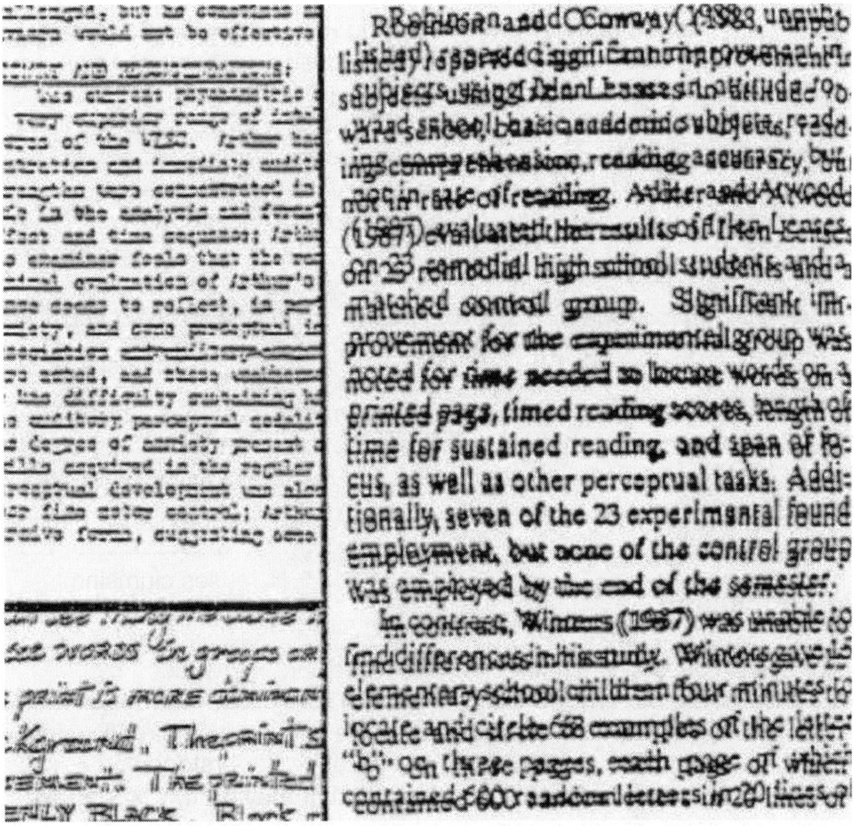

Figure 3

Some people get so used to these effects that they don't realise that it doesn't happen to everyone. Of course, it slows down the speed of reading and increases fatigue. There are some extreme examples of the way the brain can distort print information in the figure.

 For a more in-depth look at the dyslexic brain go to the General section on the CD-ROM. For more information on visual distortion go to the Reading section of the CD-ROM.

Genetics and dyslexia

Observations indicate that dyslexia seems to run in families. You may know of others in your close family with similar difficulties to you even though they may never have had dyslexia identified.

My dad was really knowledgeable. He knew a lot about everything. He read books but took ages over them. He ran his own business and did very well but he hardly ever wrote a thing down. My mum used to do all the books and write his letters until he got an accountant and a secretary.

My sister was just as clever as me but she was hopeless at exams. I went on to study science at university. She was dotty about animals and used to help the local vet, first on a voluntary basis, and then as a proper job. The vet had a lot of faith in her. She knew exactly what to do with sick animals but she couldn't be persuaded to train as a veterinary nurse. She said she was happy doing what she did and couldn't bear the thought of doing exams.

 Evidence is stacking up for a genetic connection – but not a simple one. We look a little closer at this in the Science of Dyslexia section of the CD-ROM. If you want to know some more, look for *Genetics & dyslexia* in the General section.

In conclusion

So there are several scientific explanations for problems faced by dyslexics. There are also probably many different causes for dyslexia which is why no two people have exactly the same profile of difficulties.

The major advantage of recent advances is that they show that dyslexia is very real. Many of you reading this book will have come across sceptics – people who think there is no such thing as dyslexia, that it's 'just a matter of applying yourself' and if you can't do it, then you're 'thick' or 'lazy'. Now you can say with confidence that dyslexia is real and that it is underpinned by scientific research.

We would like you to reflect on this chapter and think about the following question.

Pause

If science could produce a cure for dyslexia, would this be a good thing? Would *you* go for it? Are there any advantages to being dyslexic? Would society be poorer without dyslexic people?

In this chapter we've only been able to give you a very general overview. This means that some of the science is very over-simplified. If you have the time or energy you might like to follow up the science in one of these publications that review much of the recent research:

Dyslexia: Theory and Good Practice edited by Angela Fawcett (Whurr, 2001);
'Dyslexia in further and higher education: a framework for practice' from *Dimensions of Dyslexia V1 Assessment Teaching and the Curriculum* edited by Gavin Reid (Moray House, 1996);
Mapping the Mind by Rita Carter (Phoenix, 2000) (covers more about the workings of the brain generally).

3

Finding out about the way you learn and what you need

In this chapter we help you to find out about your needs through:

- your eyes: by reflection on how you prefer to do things;
- others' eyes: by what specialists think would be useful.

How you prefer to do things

If you hear the word 'metacognition' (meta-cog-nition), don't panic! It just means your understanding of the way you learn.

What are learning styles?
There are many kinds of learning style but they're all about how you prefer to do things. For example:

Some people prefer to work:

- on their own
- in groups
- at home
- in a reference library
- sitting at a desk
- in an armchair
- on the train
- on the beach

These are preferences about the **environment** you prefer to work in.

Some people like to work:

- with support when they need it
- with directed encouragement
- through structured courses with lessons and tutors
- through dipping into books

These are preferences about the **support** you prefer.

✐ ACTIVITY 4

You may use different styles according to the task you are tackling.
Try the following activity.

For each task tick the situation you prefer. You can print copies from the
CD-ROM, Printable document.

Tasks →	Reading the newspaper	Writing a letter	Learning how something works
In a small group of people			
Sitting at a table			
In an armchair or deckchair			
In a quiet place			
With background music			
With help			
Other (specify)			

Ask other members of your family or friends what their preferences are –
you should find that there is quite a range!

Sensory learning style
We learn by using our senses:

- seeing,
- hearing and
- doing (including smelling and touching).

When it comes to using our senses we also have a preferred way of
learning. Many people use these senses equally and often together.
These people are called 'multisensory learners'. Some people use one or
two senses more than the others. Understanding how you do things can
give you a good idea as to your preferred way of learning.

ACTIVITY 5 – Sensory learning style

There is a learning styles questionnaire on the CD-ROM Try the questions now. Print a copy from the CD-ROM, Printable document 6. Your answers will tell you more about the way you prefer to do things.

By now you should be able to identify your strengths, i.e. which sense or senses you use best. You may like to come back to this another time to see whether anything has changed.

The cognitive learning style

It's useful to think about what is called your 'cognitive' learning style. This is about the *ways* you think and deal with information. By considering the way you learn you are identifying some of your strengths. There are four main cognitive styles shown in Figure 4 below.

When looking at our cognitive learning style we consider two things:

- how we think
- how we take in and process information.

How do you think?

Do you think in words or in images such as pictures and diagrams?

If you think in words you'll be in one of the two left-hand boxes.

If you think in images, you'll be in one of the two right-hand boxes.

If you think partly in words and pictures, which do you use most? Try to decide which side of the vertical line you fall – perhaps only on one side.

The more you think in words, the more you are a 'verbaliser'.

The more you think in pictures, the more you are pictorial or 'visual'.

How do you take in and process information?

Do you take a stepwise approach, reading from start to finish, thinking things out in a systematic way? The more this applies to you, the more 'analytical' you are. You will be in one of the top two boxes.

Do you take a broad overview, an intuitive approach, see things as a whole? The more this applies to you, the more 'holistic' you are. You will position yourself in one of the two bottom boxes.

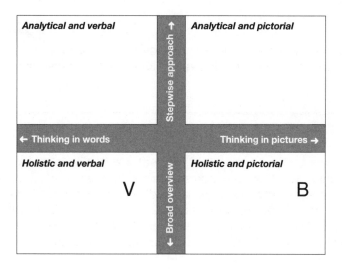

Figure 4

So which box do you fall in for both thinking and processing? Vicki is holistic and verbal, Bonita is holistic and pictorial (visual).

Figure 5 below gives you some general ideas and approaches to try for each of the four cognitive styles. These ideas are discussed in chapters 4 to 8.

Analytical and verbal	Analytical and pictorial
Try tape recorders, chanting and singing	Try visual images, videos, flow charts, wall planners
Holistic and verbal	Holistic and pictorial
Try walking about when thinking, speaking ideas onto tape, dictating to someone who can sort your ideas	Use mind maps, posters, drawings, 3-dimensional models

Figure 5

The dyslexia learning style
Dyslexic people do tend to do things differently. They are much more likely to have 'right-brained' strengths:

- thinking more holistically;
- being more intuitive – that is, seeing the answer to something but not necessarily knowing where that answer came from;
- being creative – generating lots of ideas, though they may not all be useful!

✍ ACTIVITY 6 – Left brain/right brain

Remember that the terms 'right brained' and 'left brained' are just describing ways that you approach things. It doesn't mean that if you can describe yourself as 'right brained' that the left side of the brain doesn't work. Refer back to chapter 2 for a more detailed explanation. Not all dyslexics are strongly right brained. ⊘ Try the activity in the General section of the CD-ROM if you aren't sure whether you are mainly left or right brained.

Understanding your strengths and difficulties

Metacognition – understanding how you learn

By now you should be getting a better idea of how you learn. You are developing metacognitive skills (meta-cog-nitive: *meta* is Greek for 'among, with, beside, after', and *cognitio* is Latin for 'to know').

Metacognitive skills enable us to know how we think and the processes involved in our thinking. Being aware of the way you think is extremely useful when it comes to choosing strategies.

Understanding how you are assessed

If you are dyslexic, you will probably have been assessed many times:

- as a child at school;
- again at school for exam 'concessions' or 'accommodations' – we prefer the term 'exam facilities';
- at college, university or maybe even at work;
- at an Access Centre.
- at employment centres.

In addition, you may have been 'screened' before the full assessment and you may have taken part in a reassessment to see whether your needs have changed. Try one of the helplines in appendix C.

If you have never been assessed and want to know more about the screening process go to *Screening* in the General section of the CD-ROM ☺ and/or try the helplines in Appendix C.

✍ ACTIVITY 7

Here are some questions about how you were assessed. Circle the answer that is closest to yours.

How many times have you had some form of assessment for dyslexia or 'specific learning difficulties'?	several times, once, never.
Were you (or your family) given a copy of the report?	yes, no, not sure.
Did the assessors go through it with you or your family?	yes, no, not sure.
Did you read it at the time or later?	at the time, later, never.
Did you understand it?	yes, no, not sure.

Being assessed
If you have been assessed, take a moment to assess the assessment. Answer the questions below and then read our comments. If you haven't been assessed yet or you're going to be reassessed, still look at the

comments. An assessment will include tests, observation and an interview. Ask at every stage of your assessment what the results mean and how it describes what might be going on in your brain.

- *Can you remember how long your assessment took?*
  A full assessment can be a positive and illuminating experience. It can take three hours or more and involves a lot of concentration. It can be very tiring. There is a lot to discover.
- *Can you remember what you discovered from the experience?*
  Many of the things you are asked to do are things that have given you difficulties for most of your life. It can be a very emotional experience.
- *Were the tests explained to you? Were you given an idea of what the tests were revealing as you worked through them?*
  There are some explanations in the General section of the CD-ROM.

- *Was the attitude of the assessor friendly and positive? If you were assessed as an adult, did the assessor understand your needs as an adult?*
  There is a shortage of assessors with experience of adults. This sometimes means that people feel they have been treated like a child. And when the results of tests in the report are quoted in children's ages, this seems like the final insult. Attitudes are changing. More tests specifically for adults are now available and assessors are becoming more aware of the needs of adults.
- *Did the experience touch on bad memories?*
  This is understandable. Many of you will have had bad experiences at school: working hard but seeming to get nowhere, being told you were lazy or stupid, losing interest in lessons, even playing truant. Adults often ask why their dyslexia was not identified before and feel angry because of this. If your assessment was not a fully positive experience, now is the time to put it behind you and concentrate on moving forward.
- *Was the report clear and comprehensible to you?*
  Many reports are written in technical language that other professionals cannot understand, let alone you! Ask for explanations.
- *Did you have the opportunity to discuss the report with the assessor or with someone else?*
  If possible, go back to the assessor and ask him/her to explain the findings in straightforward language. The report is, after all, **about** you and should be **for** you too.

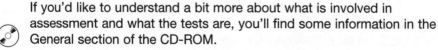

If you'd like to understand a bit more about what is involved in assessment and what the tests are, you'll find some information in the General section of the CD-ROM.

Needs assessments

Some people go to a special centre for a needs assessment. You are most likely to have had a needs assessment if you are or have been a student. Some employers will pay for such an assessment or you can pay for one yourself, but it is expensive. A needs assessor will be looking at how your particular difficulties can be best supported by technology (high, medium and low) and by people such as specialist tutors. Such an assessment is required if you wish to apply for disabled student allowances (DSAs) which are available to students in higher education to pay for equipment and support. Dyslexia is deemed to be a disability under the Disability Discrimination Act 1995.

The information in this book can help you carry out your own needs assessment. Chapters 4 to 8 give suggestions for strategies that you can use for specific purposes and adapt to suit you and your task. Chapter 9 describes some of the technology that is available.

After assessment

Pause

Well, how closely did you look at your dyslexia report when you first saw it?
Do you ever go back and look at it?
If so, for what reason?

✍ ACTIVITY 8

If you now feel that you'd like to take another look at it, try the activity in the General section of the CD-ROM, *Assessment report activity*.

What you can do

Keep a record of how you do things
☐ Make a **'How I did that'** file. It isn't only students who are learning. We all learn daily:

- in our jobs
- in voluntary work
- in sport
- listening to radio and TV
- in evening/day leisure classes

- from our children

Keep a note of how you do things. Note ways you do things that are particularly successful, but it's worth noting things that didn't work too. You probably won't want to try them again – but you might want to change what you did slightly.

For example:

Sue has difficulty finding her way to new places, particularly when she drives alone. Someone suggested that she put the directions, step by step, on post-it notes and stick them on the dashboard. This worked really well until she tore two off at once. Next time, she stuck them to the dashboard separately but overlapping so it was almost impossible to tear off two together without noticing.

She put a note in her **'How I did that'** file with a little drawing:

> *Getting things in the right order – use post-it notes, e.g. on journeys. Separate the pages first.*

Relearning things

Assessment reports often suggest 'remedial' work. It is debatable whether this is always a good thing. There is evidence that adult reading can be improved by some reading programmes and you may like to try one with a specialist tutor. But most adults find these tedious and say that they prefer to find strategies around their difficulties (see chapter 4). Some people who have a really hard time reading or writing never get up to the speed of non-dyslexic readers but they do improve significantly. More importantly they find other ways of getting there. You will find lots of ideas and suggestions for strategies in this book.

Do look (again) at the recommendations in your dyslexia report. Which ones have you done something about? Are there any that might be worth thinking about again? The next part of this book can help you with ideas.

Help, advice, guidance and counselling

If you've had dyslexia formally identified, can you remember how you felt when you were told? Many people say that they found their full dyslexia assessment a traumatic experience.

He ran up the stairs to his bedroom shouting angrily 'I won't be dyslexic, I won't!' His elder brother, also dyslexic, said reassuringly 'It's <u>good</u> to know! I was really pleased when they told me because they would know it wasn't all my fault. You will be able to get extra help and they won't yell at you for being careless.'

How did you feel when you were assessed?
Reactions are very varied – here are a few:

Relief	Tearful	Angry
Disbelief	Horror	Excited
Panic	Unhappy	Depressed
Positive	Delighted	Frustrated
Thrilled	Inspired	Emotional

Circle the ones that relate to you.

How did you or are you coping with all these emotions?
Many people who were assessed as adults have or will need to talk things over with someone. The person who assessed you may have helped you work through your feelings and explained to you what it all means. You may still want to talk to someone.

If you were assessed as a child, the talking may have been with your parents rather than with you. You may find that you need to talk to someone as an adult.

You have probably experienced all these feelings and more at some time or another. And this is understandable. Different stages in your life will produce different reactions.

The need

Which of these describes you?

☺ You have known about your dyslexia for a long time and are comfortable with it.

☺ You have known about your dyslexia for a long time and are still coming to terms with it.

☺ You have suspected that you are dyslexic for a long time but still haven't been formally diagnosed.

☺ You learned about it very recently and are greatly relieved.

☹ You learned about it very recently and are concerned about what it might mean.

It is perfectly understandable for people to have some uncomfortable feelings about their dyslexia. The reasons for this are probably related to the way the world perceives dyslexia:

• Most people aren't dyslexic and don't even understand it. Your problems are often misunderstood.

• You may have had many bad experiences – the sort of thing that is often referred to as 'baggage'.

• You may have low self-esteem following years of hostility or indifference towards your dyslexia.

• Many things may have presented huge challenges to you.

• You may have a history of failure due to lack of appropriate support.

The people in your life and the professionals you come into contact with should also understand these effects.

Whatever your situation your dyslexia will, from time to time, jump up and hit you in the face. At such times you are likely to need support:

- from your inner resources;
- from books or websites – we like to think that this book will help on many occasions;
- from people, family, friends or someone such as a counsellor who understands dyslexia.

In this section, we have given some pointers for advice, guidance and counselling that can help others to help you.

Who looks at your needs?

You

You are the most important person to consider your needs. You know yourself better than anyone else does.

The actress Susan Hampshire once wrote:

> *One of the worst aspects of being dyslexic is the vicious circle caused by stress. As soon as I make a mistake I panic, and because I panic I make more mistakes.*

Throughout this book you will find ideas for coping strategies which will help to reduce stress. You can find some specific suggestions for stress management and relaxation techniques in the General section of the CD- ROM.

If you have worked your way through this chapter and the two previous ones, you should be beginning to understand your own particular variety of dyslexia, your cognitive style, your learning style, your strengths and your weaknesses. You should also be beginning to discover what you need, to do the things you want to do.

Part 2 of this book will help you identify ideas and strategies that you can use.

Part 2

Finding the Best Way for You

There are five chapters in this section. Each one takes a different aspect of everyday tasks and suggests strategies you might like to try. Most of these strategies have been creatively devised by or with dyslexic people in various situations.

Chapter 4: Reading and the world of print
Reading strategies and activities

Chapter 5: Getting down what you want to say
Writing strategies and activities for a range of situations

Chapter 6: Getting done what you want to do
Strategies and activities for planning and organisation

Chapter 7: Handling numbers
Strategies and activities based around dealing with numbers

Chapter 8: Making memory work for you
            Developing strategies for remembering

You may want to dip into the area that gives you the most problems.
That's fine – but there are ideas in some chapters that can be adapted
for other areas. Use these ideas to devise your own strategies because
your own ideas will work best for you.

4

Reading and the world of print

Was dyslexia ever a problem before the invention of the printing press?

In this chapter we look at:

- how we got into the business of reading;
- what is involved in the process and what skills are required;
- what do you want to read;
- reading strategies;
- improving comprehension;
- help available.

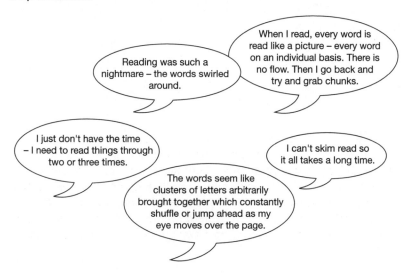

How we got into the business of reading

Today we seem to rely on print for much of our information. We seem to have forgotten that for many years, people managed without it – but that doesn't mean there were no complicated ideas or concepts. People relied on speech and oral traditions to exchange information and ideas. Migrants and travelling storytellers passed them on. Human beings, it seems, are geared up biologically for speech but not for the entirely separate and difficult business of reading and writing. Before the arrival of the printing press, intelligent and articulate people traded, invented and communicated – but mostly by word of mouth. Some people used scribes to write important letters. Writers, usually priests, were specialists but not necessarily people of influence such as kings or barons. In the same way today, government ministers employ speech writers and reports are written by civil servants. Even public examinations were conducted verbally at Oxford and Cambridge universities – there were no written examinations until the middle of the 17th century.

As the invention of the printing press rapidly increased the availability of printed materials, literacy became a skill needed by more and more people. Acquiring knowledge and information became more closely linked with the skill of decoding print – reading. Of course, handwritten documents had been around for thousands of years, but they were expensive and not available to all – the printing press made words on paper accessible to the masses! And many more people wanted and needed to read.

Mass education in the developing countries used oral teaching and learning ('rote' learning) until well into the 20th century. There was little understanding about the nature of literacy skills, so slow learning became associated with slow reading and writing.

Now, in the 21st century, print dominates our education and our access to knowledge and information. Our ability is too often measured through reading and writing. Our qualifications are mainly gained by written exams.

However, another communication revolution as great as, or greater than that of the invention of the printing press, has taken place with the introduction of computer technology. We can click and copy and paste, we can use icons, we can dictate to the machines. Producing written materials using technology is changing the way we look at reading and writing skills.

How we read

So what exactly is going on when we are reading? Have a look again at chapter 2, which explains the process of how we read in some detail. If you find this particularly interesting and want to know how we *learn* to read, then go to the Reading section of the CD-ROM. Here is a brief summary of how our brains work when we read:

	1. **Visually** We recognise familiar and short words visually – the shape of the word and the letters	2. **Phonologically** By recognising letters and groups of letters, knowing the sounds and putting them together
Examples	the of, off that, than	b – a – tch
Pitfalls	But we can confuse these and get them wrong *'I miss out the little words – I just don't see them'* Missing out 'not' can change the meaning completely!	But some letter combinations are difficult to learn because they have many different sounds or no sound at all *'The ph in physics always threw me'*

Most dyslexics have phonological difficulties so they rely more on the visual route. For example, you can recognise a word from visual cues independent of sound. You can recognise lots of words from your internal store and so can read them rapidly.

As an architect I had no problem with words like 'perspective' but I was completely thrown the first time I came across the name of the famous architect Frank Lloyd Wright in print. I had difficulty reading it.

There are other kinds of pitfalls. You can see that if you find it difficult to recognise letters or words, it can really slow you down:

- getting the letter wrong – confusing 'b' and 'd' for example;
- mistaking 'of' for 'off' or 'in' for 'on';
- missing out words or parts of words;
- getting the wrong sound for a letter or a group of letters.

But you can look for some clues to help you read. For example:

'he scored a g–––' – you don't need the other letters to guess the rest of the word correctly.

You are also using your knowledge of the *meaning* of words (semantics), for example: 'The museum visited the boy' or 'The boy visited the museum'. It is very clear from the meaning of the words 'boy' and 'museum' which sentence is correct.

The fact that letters are grouped into words helps us to read but when we speak, we run words into each other – and sometimes hesitate in the middle of a word. Without this essential clue, reading becomes very difficult. Try the following sentence:

> On ceup on atim ether eweret wobe ars

Could you decode that? Answer at the bottom of the page.*

The different spacing of the letters means you have to spend much more energy processing – and less time understanding. This is most likely to occur when reading handwriting.

We all skim over easy words helped by our word structure knowledge.

> Finished files are the result of many years of study.

How many 'f's are there in that sentence? Many people only see two at first – they miss the 'f' in the word 'of' because they only read the longer words.

* Once upon a time there were two bears

Pause

So, if learning to read is incomplete, as it is for most dyslexics, can you do anything about it now you're an adult? The pathways in your brain have become quite established. Trying to work on improving a faulty brain processing system may not be as helpful a strategy as building and extending your visual vocabulary. Do you want to spend several hours a week learning to read better or increase your reading speed? What you choose to work on depends on what you want to do.

✍ ACTIVITY 9 – How do *you* read?

Find three different things you have read today such as:

> a form
> a bit of the newspaper
> a book
> instructions about something

Look at each one and ask yourself the following questions. You might like to jot down the answers. You can print this from the CD-ROM, Printable document 15.

Item you read➜			
1. Did you read all the words?			
2. Did you hear them in your head as you read them?			
3. Did you find there were some words which you guessed the meaning of from the rest of the sentence?			
4. Did you get lost on long sentences?			
5. Did you have to reread any of them to make sure you understood what it was about?			
6. Did you notice if you took a break after a few minutes with longer texts?			
7. For how long did you read before feeling you had read enough or couldn't take in any more?			

Finally, does having to read anything more than a page fill you with dread?

Look at your answers. Are they roughly similar for each item or do you find some things easier? Which difficulties frustrate you the most? Mark these with a star as they might be worth working on. Hopefully this gives you a better idea of what reading is like for you and where you think some strategies might be useful.

We tend to read important things more carefully:

> *I read novels just following the names of the main characters and leaving out all the descriptive stuff. I couldn't read my student books like that because I had to remember and understand in a much more critical way.*

Before you look at the strategies further on, it is worth deciding what it is you would really like to read. Then you can choose the right strategy for you for that kind of reading.

You will probably end up with several strategies for different types of reading. This is called 'flexible reading' and most successful readers do it all the time. Whether you are reading study books, instructions, a report, a book about your hobby, a novel, a newspaper, you still need strategies to help make sense of the texts.

What do you want to read?

As we have said, there are many types of reading matter. We will be suggesting a number of strategies to help you improve your reading, your concentration and your comprehension. The table below summarises the strategies that you could try for different reading tasks.

 You will also need to decide whether you need to read something in detail or read it at all! Our 'Do I need to read this?' strategy can help you decide. See the Reading Section of the CD-ROM

Type of reading materials	Suggested strategies
Notices	Key words, notebook, Electronic dictionary
Letters	Encourage people to type or e-mail you
Instructions	Make them visual Record them
Newspapers	Read headlines Listen to radio or TV as alternative source of news
Reports	'Do I need to read this?' Read onto tape Make notes
Magazines/journals	Talking books Read-out computer facility
Textbooks	Read-out computer facility Use a tape Make notes
Novels	Talking books Videos Choose the right level for you

You may find other strategies that are helpful – add them to this table for future reference.

It isn't necessary to read every word, every paragraph, chapter or section – you can just read what you need for that particular occasion.

Assessing what you need to read and what you can leave out
If you have to read quite a lot you may be:

- a student;
- writing a report for work;
- working on a project;
- writing an article for a magazine.

In addition, you are likely to have to be selective in what you read.

If you are faced with too much reading you can sort it into:

essential
desirable
non-essential

 You could ask someone at work or college to give you some pointers or assistance. You can find some help on the CD-ROM in the Reading section: *Do I need to read this?*

Your toolbox: reading

This section contains some ideas that may help to improve your reading skills:

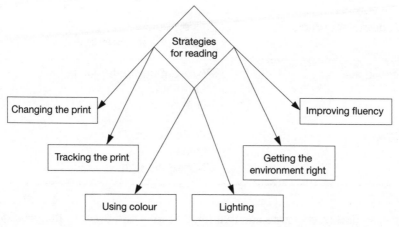

Figure 6

The print
A variety of different styles of print – called 'fonts' – are used for printing material:

Arial   Times New Roman   Courier   Comic Sans

and in a variety of sizes, measured in 'points':

9 point   14 point

Most dyslexic readers prefer fonts that are simple, without serifs (the curly bits) and a point size of about 12. It is easier for most people to read text that is only justified (lined up) on the left-hand side. You may find that you have to avoid reading certain items because the print is so unfriendly, for example when text is printed over photographs. Some of the strategies in this 'toolbox' will help to make reading easier on the eye.

Unlike the print in books and journals, you have control of the material you generate on your computer and you can ask others to help you by printing out documents:

- on the paper of your preferred colour;
- using your preferred font;
- in your preferred point size;
- left justified only.

Alternatively, they could give you the text electronically so that you can change it to suit your own specific preferences.

If you have the technology, you can scan in text and then reformat it to suit you – see chapter 9. Otherwise, if point size is a problem for some essential reading, you could try photo-enlarging (or reducing) it to suit you.

Tracking
Tracking is about how easily your eye follows the print across the page. Poor tracking is one of the most common problems that slows reading and makes comprehension difficult. Try:

- Using your finger to trace the word across the page – this has recently been suggested as a way for everyone to speed up their reading. You will see all kinds of people doing this – it's becoming fashionable!
- Use a ruler or a piece of card – not under the line you are reading but above. This will allow your eye to read on but doesn't allow it to drift back.

Lighting
The best light to read under is daylight (but not direct sunlight), so ideally you need to sit near the window. The light should fall over your shoulder but avoid shadow or glare. If you are using a desk lamp make sure it is in the right position so that the light falls on the page but doesn't cause reflections or glare. The lamp shouldn't be the only source of light in the room because too much contrast doesn't help.

Colour

Colour and lighting can make a huge difference to your reading rate and comfort. The high contrast between very white paper and black print can cause distortions and discomfort for many people. If you have trouble with reading, it may be because of visual discomfort and distortion of print on the page. A white page may seem to 'glare'. You may have a feeling of eye strain or even get headaches when you read. Words may appear to move, jumble or blur. Shadows may seem to fall on the page. All this interferes with reading, and reduces attention and concentration. For examples of what print can look like see Figure 3 in chapter 2. For more information about visual discomfort go to the Reading section of the CD-ROM.

Experiment with:

- using a highlighter pen to colour sections of text that you are finding difficult to read or understand;

- coloured overlays or tinted lenses – see the CD-Rom, *Visual discomfort*;
- different lighting conditions – type of bulb, direction of light, position of lamp or lamps (see chapter 9 for information about a variable coloured reading lamp).

The section on visual discomfort (in the Reading section of the CD-ROM contains a couple of things you can try to check whether coloured overlays might be helpful.

Getting your environment right

Sitting position – ideally for reading you need to sit fairly upright so that you are not putting pressure on your spine but on your 'sitting' bones. Sitting more upright also means a better supply of air and blood to the brain and more brain power. Your reading distance should be about 50 cm (20 in) away from your eyes to give maximum peripheral and central vision. Sitting properly, ensuring that the temperature is comfortable and that your clothes are not tight will all enhance your stamina for reading.

Distractions – absolute silence is not always the best when you are reading. You need to avoid being interrupted, but music in the background can be beneficial to concentration so experiment with this where possible. Try gentle, background music.

Improving your fluency

There are two good ways to improve your fluency in reading. One, called 'paired reading', is a great way for a friend or relative to help you. Paired reading:

- means reading aloud with someone who is a fluent reader;
- helps you to become a more fluent reader.

You read in turns and get help when you need it. Guidance on paired reading can be found in the Reading section of the CD-ROM.

The other useful method is to read at the right level for you. Choose a text with shorter sentences and very few unfamiliar words. You can work at reading a little faster if you use a slightly easier level. Alternatively you could try the SMOG method of working out the readability – this is explained in the Reading section of the CD-ROM.

People can learn to read a little quicker, sometimes a lot quicker. Furthermore, Tony Buzan, in his *Speed Reading Book*, states that this is possible for dyslexic people too. He suggests that we have to:

- push on across the page,
- and never go back.

To help increase your reading rate, try the ideas on tracking in the paragraph above.

Skimming and scanning
Skimming is different from reading quickly. It is a way of getting the general gist (idea) of something by picking out key words and ideas that catch your eye as you skim over the page. Many dyslexic people claim it is impossible for them while others are extremely good at doing this. It uses holistic strengths, i.e. getting an overall picture from various bits of information. You don't have to start at the beginning either – you can let your eye jump about, taking in those pieces of information you are drawn to. You get an overall impression of what it's all about.

It's like looking at the paintings of impressionists such as Cezanne – you know what the painting is about but you don't need to look at the detail to enjoy it.

Scanning, on the other hand, is a process of looking over some text to find a particular piece of information. You may, for example, scan something you've read in detail before going back to look for something you remember reading such as a name or date.

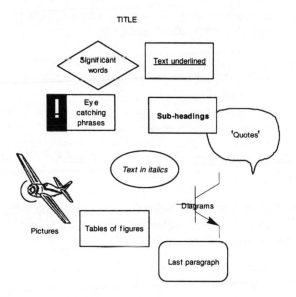

Figure 7

Your toolbox: comprehension

In this section we give you some ideas to help with your comprehension, i.e. understanding and remembering what you read:

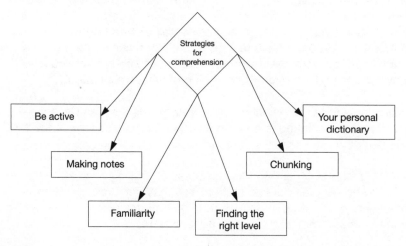

Figure 8

If you read very slowly, it can be harder to remember what you have read.

If a lot of your energy goes into working out the words, then it is hard to follow the line of thought through the sentence.

Make your reading active
To try to improve your comprehension, be an *active* reader. This also helps you to remember what you've read.

Make some short notes.

Speak a summary

- Try reading a piece of text then, without looking at it, sum it up in your own words into the tape recorder.
- Listen to what you have said with the text in front of you.

Highlighting

- As you read, underline in pencil the bits you think are important. Then choose some of these to highlight in colour.
- Put a mark in the margin to indicate something important.

Ask questions as you read

- What does the author want me to get out of this?
- Where is the author coming from – does s/he have a vested interest?
- How is this relevant?

And to help remember what you've read ...

- Tell someone about what you have read and discuss it with them.
- Act it out.
- Use the SQ3R method (Scan – Question – Read – Remember – Review). See the Reading section of the CD-ROM.

Making notes
Note making is a helpful strategy. It makes your reading active and you can keep the notes as a permanent record if necessary. Making notes:

- keeps you concentrating;
- aids your understanding of what you are reading by putting it into your own words;
- helps you to organise your thinking;
- makes you identify the main points;
- helps you to remember what you have read;
- gives you something to refer back to that is shorter and more concise.

You can find ideas of ways to make notes in chapter 5 (Notemaking section) and in the Writing section of the CD-ROM.

Practise making notes:

1. Choose a general easy text to practise on.
2. Identify the main issues and any new vocabulary.
3. Try making a mind map or diagram – see chapter 5 (Making a plan section).

Using familiarity

It is a lot easier to read about a subject that you are familiar with. If you want to learn more about a new topic, try to find a children's book on the subject, a basic book or some introductory information on the Internet or in a magazine. Children's books, such as those published by Usborne for example, are particularly useful because they are written for less experienced readers – information is often expressed in simpler sentences and well-chosen vocabulary. This makes it easier to cope with new words. Once the new vocabulary becomes more familiar and the basic ideas are clearer, you can move on to a more detailed text. Many children's texts are simply better written – they have fewer unnecessary words or long complex sentences that add nothing to the meaning but make it harder to understand for dyslexic readers in particular. Failing that, an encyclopaedia is a good starting point.

Personal dictionary

Copy into an address book those words you would like to keep for handy reference. There won't be many words, so finding them will not be too difficult even if your sense of alphabetical order is unreliable.

You could include:

- Useful words that you tend to stumble over or forget the meaning of such as 'accommodation', 'deference', 'psychology', 'mnemonic' etc. You can also use it for words you have difficulty spelling such as 'school', 'business', 'necessary' etc.
- Names of people you may need to write to at work.
- Words that you have to use in your work, your hobbies or your studies.

 You can find some examples in the Spelling section of the CD-ROM.

Chunking

Read in meaningful chunks. You can, for example, read everything under one sub-heading and take a break before going on to the next.

- Read the title, headings and first and last paragraphs or sections to get an overview.
- Read a paragraph at a time, pause after each and ask yourself – what was that mainly about?
- Take regular breaks.

Using time and taking breaks

Find your best concentration time. This can vary from person to person, from day to day and for different times of the day. On average, we cannot maintain a high level of concentration for more than about 20 minutes. So, if you are reading something that is quite demanding, make sure you take regular breaks.

Try reading for 15 or 20 minutes:

- make a few summary notes,
- have a quick stretch or get a drink,
- then go on to the next section.

You can always use any odd minutes you find you have spare. Use short chunks of free time to prepare for a larger reading task:

- get all the reading material together in one place;
- make sure you have other things you need: soft pencil, highlighter, notepaper, tape recorder, ruler, dictionary;
- go through the piece and decide which sections you need to read.

Now you are well prepared to start the task when you have more time.

Reading aloud

In our opinion, no one should ever be put in the position of having to read aloud but sometimes it is unavoidable. Problems often stem from school where, it seems, children may have to read aloud in front of others.

> I hated being asked to read out loud at school as I was so anxious about pronouncing the words correctly.

> I used to play truant on days where we had to read out loud to the class.

> I used to try and memorise the whole passage so I could read my bit.

Although it is generally thought that this is only a major problem for young dyslexics at school, comments from dyslexic adults suggest that the problem persists into adulthood.

I worried about tutorials in case I had to read a bit out.

I hate meetings, in case I have to read bits aloud.

Reading aloud to adults
Employing strategies for reading aloud are more limited unless you tell people that you are dyslexic or have a reading difficulty. If you know beforehand that you will have to read something aloud you can:

- at least prepare your bit and practise;
- read it onto tape so that you can hear it;
- even try to memorise it – for ideas on memorising see chapter 8;
- before a meeting, offer to do a particular part so you are in control of your contribution.

Reading to children
Don't feel you can't do this – there's magic in turning over pages together.

- Practise first on their favourite books – you could then record them on tape.
- Listen to the tapes together.
- Use talking books and listen together.

This can be fun and you'll be reading at a lower level which will help you to improve your fluency. Poetry can be easier: poems such as those by Dr Seuss are rhythmic, repetitive, good for your phonological awareness (see chapter 1) and children love them!

Sir Steve Redgrave (Olympic oarsman and also dyslexic):
Now that I have children, I want to make sure that they can read and write well. I spend a lot of time reading to them and, as a result, my own reading has improved too.

If you still feel a bit nervous about reading to children, do what people did before books – use your imagination and make up stories.

Using a library

Don't be overwhelmed by the size, arrangement and the number of books. Although all libraries are slightly different they have basically the same layout, i.e. they are divided up into sections according to topics.

Fiction books are filed in alphabetical order by the author's surname so take your alphabet arc with you (CD-ROM, printable documents 4). You may find that science fiction has a subsection of its own, as does poetry.

Non-fiction will be divided up into subsections such as Travel, Science, Hobbies, etc. These will be further divided; for example, travel will be divided into continents and then subdivided into countries.

You will probably find oversize books on the bottom shelf – below where they would be if they weren't so big! The title and author's name will be printed on the spine but there is no standard style. The print can be read with your head over to the left or to the right or, sometimes, the print is horizontal. If you are skimming along a shelf this can make you feel quite dizzy.

The reference section can be very useful for encyclopaedias, directories, newspapers, journals, brochures, CD-ROMs etc. but you can't borrow these – they have to be read in the library.

Our advice is to treat the library much as you would a department store or supermarket; if you can't find what you want, ask for help. Most libraries have electronic indexes on a computer. For example, if you're looking for an article in a journal, take a quick look at the index and then ask if you can't find it. If you are going to use the library a lot, ask for guidance on how to use the index. You can also ask for a printed copy of the instructions so that you can refer to them again.

Libraries can be complicated places. Most people, dyslexic or not, have to ask for help at some time.

Borrowing books from public libraries is free. If they don't have the book you are interested in, you can ask them to get it for you from another library. Libraries give you the opportunity to read books you don't want to buy, read books you might want to buy and read books that are no longer available to buy. They are very good value!

In this chapter we have looked at:

* Why we need to read.

- The processes involved in reading summarised from chapter 2.
- The kind of problems that can make reading difficult.
- Strategies to help you with reading and comprehension.
- Reading aloud and using a library.

We hope that you can now:

- Understand a bit more about how you read and what you need to read.
- See how you can be more selective in what you read.
- Find ways to improve your comprehension.
- Get more enjoyment from your reading.

5

Getting down what you want to say

Writing is easy. All you do is stare at a blank sheet of paper until drops of blood form on your head (Gene Fowler, journalist).

In this chapter we look at:

- the tasks involved in writing;
- how you can break it down into smaller more manageable chunks;
- strategies that can help you, many of which have been devised by dyslexic people;
- what help is available.

Where do you start?

You have something you need to write. You also have lots of ideas and a blank sheet of paper. Where do you start?

Why might writing be difficult for you?

Writing is a complex task – in fact, it is a complex collection of tasks. These tasks need to be broken down to get started.

The writing task

What is different about spoken and written language?
Spoken language is different from written language. Some of these differences are very subtle. If you get the chance, look at a written transcript of spontaneous speech.

Here is Jimmy Tarbuck talking about George Harrison:

> *He used to play his guitar . . . and he'd have a cigarette on one of the strings . . . er . . . you know . . . when they tie the string to top of the guitar and the strings would be loose . . . he'd sometimes have a cigarette . . . and he was . . . um . . . a heavy smoker when he was younger.*

In speech we shorten phrases such as 'he would' to 'he'd' and we add expressions such as 'you know'. We may also wave our hands about, use different voice tones, put emphasis on words and make facial expressions to help convey the meaning. These options are not available when we write things down so we need to use other ways of conveying meaning:

- put words together in sentences so that the meaning is clear;
- use punctuation to help make points clear or for emphasis.

The words are not so very different.
The ideas are the same.
It is the *conventions* that are different. Writing is more complex.

Breaking down the task

Why is writing complex?
Just consider all the things you have to think about:

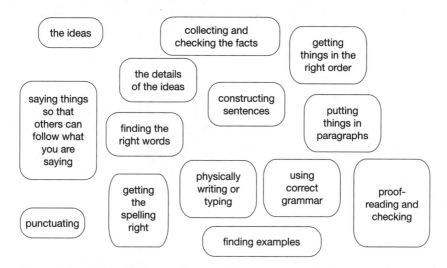

Figure 9 Tasks involved in writing – can you think of any more?

✍ ACTIVITY 10

Figure 9 shows that there are a lot of tasks to cope with! But you don't have to tackle them all at once. Some of these tasks are creative and others are about the conventions of writing. Try sorting them into two groups. We have done a couple for you:

Creative Tasks	**Conventions**
The details of the ideas	Punctuating

You can check your answers against our list below.

We group the tasks like this:

Creative tasks	Conventions – transcribing your work
The ideas	Physically writing or typing
The details of the ideas	Constructing sentences
Collecting and checking the facts	Saying things so that others can
Finding examples	follow what you are saying
Getting things in the right order	Finding the right words
	Getting the spelling right
	Putting things in paragraphs
	Punctuating
	Proof-reading and checking
	Using correct grammar

Pause

Now you should have some understanding of what writing is and what it can involve.

You have discovered that writing is, in fact, two separate groups of tasks:

Composition *and* Transcription

1. Composition is *creative*: the gathering of ideas, selecting words and getting it all on paper in fluent sentences and paragraphs.	2. Transcription is based on *conventions*: the physical act of writing grammatically.

It is best to concentrate on the creative tasks first – don't worry about spelling, punctuation, grammar etc. until you have put all your ideas down on paper.

If it helps, you can also forget about the act of writing by using a tape recorder!

What do you want to write?
Everyday life involves lots of writing tasks. The following table lists some of the more common writing tasks and some ideas for strategies to use. Most of the rest of the chapter looks at strategies that dyslexic people have found useful. Think of these as tools in your writing toolbox. Try

them out and adapt them to suit you. First we'll look at handling **your ideas**, then we'll look at the **conventions**.

Use this table to help you identify the strategies you could use for a particular task.

Writing task	Strategies to try
Memos and messages e-mails	Bullet points Templates Spell checker
Keeping records	Use symbols to represent things
Letters: formal, informal, congratulations, condolences, lobbying, to the local paper, complaints, job applications Completing forms	Making simple plans Recording ideas on tape Using samples or templates Spelling and grammar checkers Read questions and your answers aloud onto tape
Curriculum vitae (CV) References for people	Using samples or templates Planning Recording ideas on tape
Minutes of meetings	Using samples or templates
Presentations	Planning Recording ideas on tape
Articles: for a club magazine or in-house newspaper Reports: for work, for your interest groups, for a pressure group Essays, dissertations and theses	Planning Recording ideas on tape Templates Spelling and grammar checkers

Your toolbox: some strategies to help with writing

If you are finding your writing task overwhelming, it's probably a complex piece: a difficult letter, an essay or a report. The task needs breaking down. You can use the ideas in this section for all kinds of writing but they are especially useful for more complicated work.

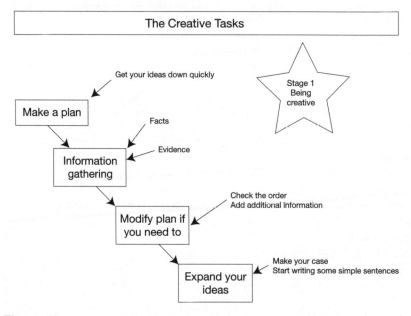

Figure 10

Figure 10 shows you the various stages in the creative side of your writing. Use this to identify the stages that you need to go through and which we will describe.

Note making supports the creative task. You need notes as a way of keeping your information handy rather than collected in lots of books open at different pages. You need notes to summarise your ideas but they do not have to involve a lot of writing (see the section on note making later in this chapter).

☆ Make a plan
Whatever the writing task, having a plan will make it easier. All written work should be planned even if the task is straightforward and the plan simple. Planning helps to break down the task of doing something you don't like doing or are finding overwhelming. This is the most important stage and it is well worth spending the extra time.

Getting your ideas down
1. Try capturing your ideas quickly on tape.
2. You can capture your ideas directly onto paper by just jotting them down as they occur to you – or you can transfer them from your tape.
3. If you like working on a computer, use planning software (see chapter 9) to capture your thoughts.

Getting your ideas sorted
The next stage is to get your ideas sorted. You'll probably want to try out several different structures to find the right one. Group your ideas together logically and in a sensible order.

1. If your ideas have been recorded on one large sheet of paper, you can use colour highlighters to sort them – a different colour for each topic.
2. If you used post-it notes, then you can group them together on a large sheet of paper, table or even a wall. Each group should have a common theme or topic.
3. If you are using planning software, this will also help you collect similar ideas together.

If you find a blank sheet of paper scary – don't start with one. Keep a supply of blank spider or tree diagrams, or a blank list like those in Figure 11 to help start you off – use whatever works best for you. You can print some from the CD-ROM.

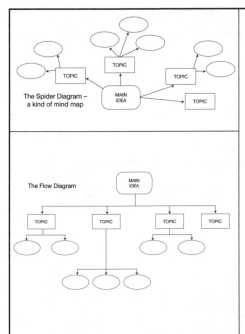

The **spider diagram** works best for people who think in pictures and who may not be very good at getting things in the right order first time. Spider diagrams are a type of **mind map**. Start with the main idea in the middle. Then divide this up into all the topics you can think of (you can number them later). Link the topics to the main idea with arrows. Then think about how you can subdivide each topic (CD-ROM, Printable document 10).

The **flow diagram** has a bit more structure to it than the spider diagram (CD-ROM, Printable document 11).

Letter to my MP about recycling rubbish
1. Intro – Gov not doing enough
2. Amount of household rubbish
   – figures and stats
   – incinerators
   – number of landfill sites
3. Unnecessary packaging
   – increase
   – attitudes
4. Materials that can be recycled
   paper/glass/metals/batteries
5. Conclusion – need proper policy.
	The **list** approach is good for people who like to do things in sequence (CD-ROM, Printable document 12).

	There are more ideas and examples for these planning tools on the CD-ROM as well as some blank charts for you to use.

Figure 11

Don't forget that you will also need to think about your introduction and conclusion – even a letter needs to have these, though they will probably be very short.

You don't have to follow these ideas, or the others in this chapter, like a slave. Adapt them to suit you and the way you think and work!

☆ **Information gathering**
Note that we have put 'planning' first. You don't have to get the information together before planning! Having a plan helps you to identify the information you need, so use your plan to guide you.

If you have used colour coding for each topic on your plan, you can use the same colour scheme to mark the information. The information can be kept in matching coloured folders.

☆ **Modify your plan and add detail**
You may want to alter your plan at this stage for various reasons:

- You have found some information that doesn't fit into your plan.
- You find you need to divide one of your topics into two or more topics.

Now is the time to consider making changes:

- Check back to your original task – are you still on the right track?
- Check that your topics are in the right order.

☆ Expanding your ideas

Now you have your plan and some notes, you can begin to expand on your ideas to include more detail if you feel it necessary.

- Take each topic separately. Make a list of relevant points using phrases or short sentences.
- Expanding simple sentences: try writing short sentences to begin with, each covering one point. You may find it easier to write these as a list first to make sure that you include all the details. If you find this difficult, record it on a tape first.

Backing up what you are saying
In some writing tasks you will need to make a case for something:

- in a letter of complaint;
- in an job application – as evidence of your capabilities;
- in a memo – to ensure that people act on your request;
- in record keeping – so that you or others will know why a decision was made;
- in a reference you write about someone.

Making sure that you have made a good case needs a few simple strategies. We give some ideas in the table below. There are more detailed ideas for *Making a case* in the Writing section on the CD-ROM. Make sure you have all the facts for backing up your case.

Your case should:	*Strategies to use:*
• be consistent	*Check there are no contradictions in what you say*
• explain any evidence that you are using	*Say where you found the evidence*
• distinguish between fact and opinion	*Ask yourself: can it be proved or is it just an opinion?*

Pause

By now we hope you can see that the writing task can be broken down into **creative tasks** and **transcription tasks.** You should feel that you can forget the transcription tasks and just concentrate on getting and organising the ideas first.

Your toolbox: some more strategies to help with writing

The conventions

The conventions broadly cover all the transcription tasks – the different stages involved in getting our ideas down on paper in a way that they can be understood clearly by others. Thinking about these tasks can get in the way of ideas, so don't concentrate on grammar, spelling, punctuation etc. until you are happy that you have collected most of your ideas together.

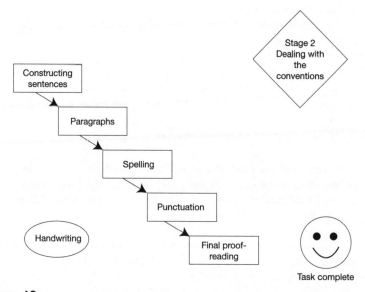

Figure 12

 Here we give you some ideas for transcription strategies to start with – there are more in the Writing section of the CD-ROM.

✧ Constructing sentences
If you have followed the strategies suggested so far, you will have most, if not all, of the points you want to make in your planning diagram. This was part of being creative – composing what you want to say.

A tape recorder can be very useful as it allows you to rehearse what you want to say. Let the tape run and try saying things in different ways, then copy down the best version.

Sentences should have a subject and a verb ...

Subject – a noun or a pronoun	Verb
The Prime Minister *They* *The ship*	*spoke.* *were running.* *will sail.*

... but will usually include much more.

If you think you have difficulty writing grammatically correct sentences, make them simple first. Then you can add more detail by using different parts of speech that are described in the table:

Basic parts of speech	
noun	A word that is the name of a person, thing or quality: ***Prime Minister, ship, computer, John, idea***
pronoun	A word used in place of a noun usually to avoid repeating the noun: *It, they, you, him* *The ship will sail. It leaves on Monday.*
verb	A word that expresses an action or a state. It is a 'doing' or 'being' word: ***spoke, were running, stands***
adjective	A word used to describe a noun or pronoun: *old, pretty, blue, large* *The **large** ship will sail.*
adverb	A word used with a verb to add to or modify the meaning: *quickly, softly, pleasantly* *They were running **quickly.***

 You can find more *Parts of speech* on the CD-ROM in the Writing section.

✧ Paragraphs
Paragraphs need:

* <u>one</u> central theme or idea;
* to start with a <u>pointer</u> sentence that answers the question: What is this paragraph all about?

Everything in the paragraph <u>must</u> relate to its central theme. Finish with a concluding sentence that:

Either ... summarises or sums up the paragraph
Or... leads on to the next paragraph.

Here is a visual reminder of what a paragraph should look like:

What is this paragraph all about?

Discussion
Arguments
Examples
Evidence
All relating to the theme of the paragraph

Summary of the paragraph or trailer for next paragraph

There are two important paragraphs to remember: the introduction and conclusion.

Almost every piece of writing needs an introduction and conclusion – many people find it easier to write the introduction last!

The introduction should tell your reader what you are intending to say. The conclusion should briefly summarise what you have said and link to your introduction. It might also say something about what you think is the next step, such as future action to be taken by someone else.

✧ Spelling

Spelling only became rule-bound in the 18th century. Before then, people were much less concerned with spelling consistently. Not so long ago, the majority of people couldn't write, so spelling wasn't an issue.

Spelling is one of the biggest worries for dyslexic people, partly due to bad memories of school but mainly because, unfortunately, people are often judged by the way they spell. Most people are imperfect spellers or make mistakes when under pressure. Here are some strategies you can use to help to improve your spelling:

- Find out some of the more common spelling rules. Which ones give you problems? Find creative ways to remember them.
- Make words visual in some way to help imprint a spelling on your mind.
- Use mnemonics (a rhyme, a pun, anything that helps you to remember – see chapter 8) to remind you of difficult spellings.
- Make a bookmark on stiff paper or card and write key words on it. This is useful for jargon or technical words.
- Your personal dictionary – collect words you want to learn in an address book or on index cards. Keep it in your pocket and refer to it when you have a spare minute.
- Try using a spelling dictionary such as the *Ace* (see appendix b) which groups words by how they sound.
- Use a spell checker – hand-held or on a computer.
- Write words you use regularly on large pieces of paper with brightly coloured pens and stick them up around the house.

For more about these strategies with examples, including a Multisensory Spelling Programme for Priority Words (MUSP), see the Spelling section of the CD-ROM.

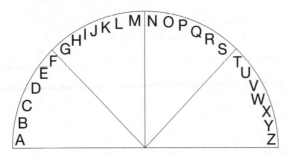

If you have difficulty looking words up in dictionaries and other reference books that are arranged in alphabetical order, try an alphabet arc. It can be kept folded up in your pocket for quick reference. This is one of the most popular strategies used by the dyslexic adults we know. You can print a copy from the CD-ROM, Printable document 4.

✧ **Punctuation**

✎ ACTIVITY 11 – Why is punctuation important?

Take a moment to think why punctuation might be important.

Read the following passage and see if you are right:

bill and jane are going to paris on tuesday for a long weekend it will be their first visit so they have bought several guidebooks to give them an idea of what to see jane says bill won't want to spend too much time in art galleries but they both agree that the louvre is essential

Punctuation:

- Makes things easier to read.
  For example, even if we are not good at punctuation, we expect to see capital letters in the right places: *Bill and Jane are going to Paris on Tuesday.*
- Makes the meaning clear.
  Who won't want to spend too much time in art galleries?
  Jane says Bill won't want to spend too much time in art galleries.
  Jane, says Bill, won't want to spend too much time in art galleries.

.	full stop (stop or period)
?	question mark
,	comma
!	exclamation mark
'	apostrophe
( )	brackets
" "	quotation marks
–	dash
:	colon
;	semicolon

So we can see that punctuation is important for the reader. We <u>expect</u> punctuation and feel uncomfortable if it is missing or incorrect.

Thinking too much about punctuation as you write is likely to get in the way of ideas and interfere with the flow. The first three in the table are the most important so here is some advice about using them.

(⊘ For further advice go to the Punctuation section of the CD-ROM.)

. Full stop (stop or period)
Full stops mark the end of a sentence. Use them more than you expect to – if you are in any doubt use a full stop. This helps to avoid long rambling sentences.

Full stops should be used with abbreviations: e.g., p.t.o. They are often dropped in common abbreviations, particularly those with capital letters (called acronyms): BBC, MP, AA, EU.

? Question mark
Use a question mark every time there is a genuine direct question:

Are you going? but not in reported questions: *I asked if he was going.*

, Commas
A comma indicates a slight pause in a sentence. Like twins, they often come in pairs so that they can separate out ideas in a sentence. But don't include too many in your sentence – if in doubt, use a full stop.

- To separate out something that isn't essential to the sentence:
  Hamlet, *a tragedy by Shakespeare, is a long play.*
- To separate items in a list:
  My journey will take me through France, Belgium, the Netherlands and Germany.
- To separate out the conditional part of the sentence:
  If you do that, you will miss the bus.
  After we've been to the shops, we can have a cup of coffee.
- To separate out a word which links to the previous sentence:
  However, next year is a leap year. Next year is a leap year, however.

So you can think of commas as being separators.

Capital letters
Use capital letters:

- At the start of each sentence.

- For a person's name: Vicki, Mrs Robinson, Dr Thomson.
- Trade names and businesses: Woolworths.
- Names of places: East Wittering, Paris, Germany.
- Streets and rivers: 10 Downing Street, River Wye.
- Days and months: Friday 19th May.
- Titles of specific people, organisations, events, courses: the Prime Minister, Friends of the Earth, the General Election, Pure Mathematics.
- Abbreviations: BBC, USA.

> The best time to check the punctuation is after you have finished most of the writing.

✧ Proof-reading – checking what you have written

Proof-reading and correcting your errors should be done last. When you're satisfied with the content and structure, read through your draft at least twice – once to check spelling and once for punctuation.

It can be very difficult to spot your own errors, especially if dyslexia affects your visual perception. So here are some strategies to try:

- Read your work several times over and concentrate on something different each time: spelling, paragraphing, punctuation.
- You could try reading your work backwards from the end to the beginning, word by word. You'll spot many of your mistakes and notice words you're not sure of.
- If you are proof-reading on your computer screen, enlarge the font size to 150 as errors seem to stand out better.
- Correct errors immediately you spot them. Note in the margin any words you think you might have spelt wrongly. Then ask someone for advice or use a dictionary to correct these.
- Read your work from the beginning and look for errors related to your particular difficulties, for example: omitted words, wrong punctuation, incorrect grammar.
- Try reading your work onto a tape and playing it back. You're likely to *hear* anything that doesn't make sense.
- Get someone else to proof-read as well.

Breaking down the proof-reading task
Spread the proof-reading over more than one day – several, if possible. Mistakes that you miss on one day often seem to stand out on another. You can print a comprehensive *Checklist for proofreading* from the CD-ROM, Printable document 13.

✧ Handwriting

The task we need to think about while we transcribe our ideas is handwriting. Many people use word processors these days and this is generally good news for dyslexic people – it makes what you write legible for others as well as for you. But you may not have a computer to hand. Your handwriting may be good but it may take you a long time. Many dyslexic people do not join up letters. They print because they know that everyone will be able to read it. They have never really mastered the art of joined-up writing.

If your handwriting needs improving, if your hand tires when you write for any length of time or if you try to avoid handwriting, here are a few ideas to help:

- Try different kinds of pen (ballpoint, fibre-tip etc.) and colours. Try fatter or thinner pens. Try changing to a different pen while you are writing – a different-shaped pen will use different muscles and help to relieve the strain. Try a pen that flows more easily like some fibre-tips. Experiment to find the sort that suits you best.
- If you find it hard to keep the size and shape of the letters regular, look for a basic book on handwriting. Try the Handwriting activity.
- Use squared paper to help keep your writing even.
- Pull the pen over the paper, rather than push it. There's less resistance that way.

A word processor will, of course, spare you the difficulties of handwriting as well as helping to avoid spelling errors. Learning to touch-type can be very useful as many words become automatic by locating the letters to the position of the fingers.

Pause

You should now appreciate that it isn't necessary to think about the conventions of writing until you have collected and ordered all your ideas. You now have a 'toolbox' of strategies and suggestions to deal with

> constructing sentences
> constructing paragraphs
> spelling
> punctuation
> checking or proof-reading
> handwriting

that have worked for many people. You can adapt these to suit you and the task you have in hand. We want to encourage you to create your own strategies – don't feel that you have to do things the way you were taught if these haven't worked in the past. Try something new.

Pause – something to think about

Perhaps you'll get to grips with all the conventions and get all the transcription right, but remember – it means nothing without the good ideas.

Colourless green ideas sleep furiously.

Written work can be perfect, grammatically clear and concise – and totally without meaning – as Professor Noam Chomsky demonstrates in the sentence above!

Note making: a particular kind of writing skill

This is a good moment to look at how to make notes – many of the strategies can also be used for planning and writing. Notes don't have to be – and shouldn't be – as 'wordy' as the text on this page for example. Your notes can be more visual and diagrammatic. You can use colour and abbreviations.

Here are some ideas – you can mix and match them to suit the occasion:

1. Mind maps: on a separate sheet of paper, pick out the key points as words, phrases or short sentences. For more on how to make mind maps see the Writing section on the CD-ROM.	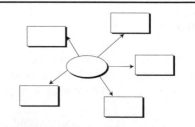
2. Marking text, either by underlining or highlighting: use a highlighter pen to mark key words and phrases.	You have to be very selective – otherwise you'll highlight everything! This is a bit like finding you can't get everything into your suitcase – what are the essentials?

3. Summing up each paragraph in one sentence.	This takes practice – but combine it with the next idea ...
4. Use a tape recorder.	Say in your own words what you think you have understood from what you have just read. Imagine that you are telling someone about it – but you haven't got much time so you have to give them the general gist.
5. Question as you go – your notes can be the answers to your questions.	How? What? Why? Where? Who?

Use your preferred learning style (see CD-ROM, Printable document 6). Which learning style does each of the ideas above use? [1. Seeing. 2. Seeing. 3. Doing. 4. Hearing. 5. Doing.]

You may need to make notes:

- in meetings;
- at talks or lectures;
- from radio or TV;
- from books.

In the first three situations you will have very little time to make notes, let alone practise some strategies. If there is a handout – add notes to this. You have more time if you are making notes from books – so start practising making notes as you read using one or more of the strategies. This will help you to improve your concentration and comprehension while learning how to make notes at the same time. Note making is also a particular kind of reading skill. Try using a spider diagram, adding a new leg for each new topic. Try developing your own abbreviations as a kind of shorthand. Try using visual diagrams such as stars, arrows, simple drawings. Only write down one or two word memory joggers.

Possible sources of help with writing

Help from people
Here are some ideas as to how other people can help including close friends, family, tutors and workmates. You don't have to tell anyone that you are dyslexic if you don't want to. You can just ask them to do specific things because

this helps me to get things clearer in my mind

or

this is the way my brain works.

- To help get your ideas down, ask someone to write down the gist of what you are saying. There is no need to dictate as that is a skill in itself. Find someone who can write fast or do shorthand and who can capture the feel for what you are saying.
- Ask someone to check your work. If you know the person well you can ask them not to do the corrections but just to indicate any errors for you to find and correct – this is a good learning exercise. If you are a student you could ask your tutor to mark part or all of your work like this. We have included an Error Analysis Checking handout on the CD-ROM for this purpose (Printable document 14).

Computers

Word-processing packages on computers can help you cope with many tasks you might find difficult or time-consuming. Maybe you haven't tried using one yet because:

- you feel that you aren't technically minded or
- you can't afford it.

Well, technology isn't everything, but chapter 9 gives you an idea of what is available. A computer can be a real boon for writing tasks. Consider the following benefits for writing and try out some of the suggestions:

- It compensates for your overloaded working memory because you can get things down quickly.
- You can move text around easily – there is no need for endless rewriting.
- Your text is legible, neat and you don't have to think about letter formation.
- Inbuilt spell checkers correct most spelling errors and many grammatical errors too.
- Voice-activated software can type in the words as you speak – see chapter 9.

These are only some of the benefits but don't just take our word for it. There are a number of places that you can try out equipment without pressure – see chapter 9.

These are only some of the benefits but don't just take our word for it. There are a number of places that you can try out equipment without pressure – see chapter 9.

Pause

Look at these two statements. Which would you prefer to hear?

Here is a terrible piece of work – look at the spelling and punctuation!

This is quite an interesting piece of work – quite a few typos though!

Both statements were made by the same person about the same piece of work. The first piece of work was handwritten; the second was typed but had exactly the same errors (typos).

Other sources of help

There are many sources of published sample letters, reports, CVs, references. You can find such samples or templates in books or on websites. A template gives you an outline for you to fill in your own details. Ask in a good bookshop or search on the Internet.

Some professional writers or scribes will, for a fee, write down from your dictation. Ghost writers will write the text in their own words from what you tell them.

All writing tasks can be difficult.

The art of writing is the art of applying the seat of the pants to the seat of the chair (Mary Vorse, author).

We hope that by reading this chapter you now feel that, funny though this quote is, there are many more ways of recording your ideas than just sitting and staring at a blank piece of paper.

In this chapter you should:

- have gained a better understanding of what writing involves;
- be able to break down the task into smaller, more manageable tasks;
- have tried some new strategies to help with writing;
- be aware of the help that is available.

6

Getting done what you want to do

Being organised helps you wrestle back the controls from life

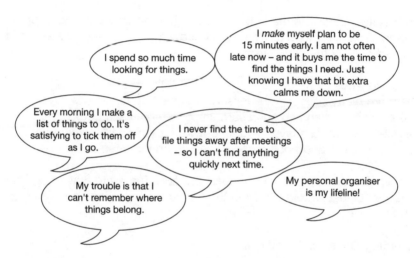

In this chapter we look at some ideas for organising time and things you may have to get done. You will see that a lot of the strategies are similar to many of the ideas discussed in previous chapters. You should be getting the feeling that strategies fall into groups with common themes: multisensory, chunking, making things memorable, etc. This should help you when you are trying to think of ways to do things or how to begin a task.

How you do things now

✍ ACTIVITY 12 – Finding out what works for you

In this activity we want to help you identify some of the organisational skills you use successfully and some of the things you leave to chance.

Think of an occasion when you had to meet a deadline. For example:

- getting the car ready for its MOT;
- getting to a new destination on time;
- making a wedding cake;
- filling in your tax form;
- organising a birthday party;
- going on holiday.

Jot down your answers to the following questions. You can print a table for this activity from the CD-ROM, Printable document 8. You may find it useful to do this activity more than once, for example, for something that worked well and for something that was a bit of a disaster. You can then compare your answers for both.

What planning did you do to ensure that you met the deadline?
What materials did you use?
Who else was involved?
How did you make sure that they did their part?
Did you meet the deadline?
If not, what went wrong?
What would you do next time to make things work better?

Take some time to answer the last question. You'll need to look at your answers to the others first. You may not be able to come up with the right ideas straight away, but read on and then come back to the question to see if some of the things we suggest can be adapted to suit you

Pause

Why don't things go right? Look at these quotes from dyslexic people. What is the feeling common to them all?

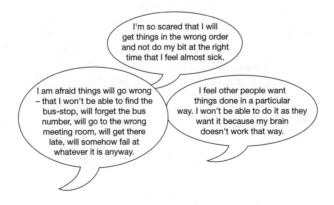

The answer is fear. There are all sorts of reasons why you cannot seem to get organised. Fear of failure, lack of confidence, concerns about making things worse – all these can stop you making a start. Sometimes it is the fear of it all seeming too much. This is the fear of the holistic person! All the tasks we have to do rush into our heads all at once – to make sense of them we have to put them in order. Think about the strategies suggested in previous chapters and take a moment to think about which strategies would be useful here.

One of the best approaches involves

- Chunking – breaking down the task into smaller tasks.
- Planning – getting them in the right order.

These get you started and ensure some success.

Two accounts of difficulties with organisation
1 Dealing with new equipment

Most people don't read instructions or those lengthy computer manuals. They work it out as they go. Are they simply impulsive or is their learning style that they learn best by 'doing'?

Here is one person's account of the struggle to cope with instructions:

I'm afraid to read instructions in case I can't follow them. Unless they are printed in fairly large letters and they don't look too long or complicated, my brain seems to tell me that I won't be able to follow them.

So I 'dash' at the task, pressing every button on the computer in the vain hope it will do as I want. And yes, it is true that if I slow down and calmly talk myself into looking it up and writing down in a list what I have to do first – then I can help myself.

It has taken me so many painful experiences and occasional observation to realise that organisation is worthwhile. I am enthusiastic and impatient and just dash at things – sometimes with wonderful intuitive expertise! But it isn't the way to get the better of technology.

Here are some ideas that could help:

- Put those boring manuals in one place so that you can find them in a year or so.
- Set time aside to spend on that manual – not the most riveting of reading, so a short period per day over a few days will suffice.
- Highlight the bits that look useful to you and try things out – learn by doing.
- If the information is available electronically (and many manuals are these days), change the font and the background colour to suit you.
- Try writing your own instructions as you go – in your own words rather than in technical jargon.

These ideas break down the task and get things in the right order.

2 Dealing with a new journey
And here is another person who has made some attempt to get organised, despite her real fears:

For me it is directions. I hurl myself into the car to drive somewhere knowing I don't really know the way – but fearing to try and work it out first from a map.

I have finally asked friends to e-mail me directions to their houses. I put these and any notes I have on scraps into a thin folder. I put the folder in the car in the big road-map book. Then when I panic a bit, I pull over and look through the folder.

- Set aside some time to look at the road or street map.
- Trace your route with a highlighter if possible. Look for possible landmarks such as crossroads, churches, railway bridges.
- Use Multimap or Streetmap on the Internet. If you know the postcode the software will point to the exact place.
- Write down each movement in the right order. Get help if you find maps difficult.
- Alternatively, ask someone to give you directions; clear written directions, a new one on each line, with landmarks indicated. Verbal directions could be recorded on tape to be played back in the car or on a personal stereo.
- For car journeys, transfer the instructions onto large post-it notes – one or two per note. Stick them on the dashboard and peel them off as you go.
- Estimate the time it is going to take you. For car journeys you can use the AA and RAC websites to help with this.

> Take time to plan and prepare. Break the task down into smaller tasks. Get things in the right order.

Organising time

Many tasks take dyslexic people longer to complete, particularly those involving reading and writing.

✍ ACTIVITY 13

Do you know exactly how long it takes you to do particular tasks? Time a few tasks and keep a note. Try some of these. Estimate the time – then time yourself and see if you are right.

Task	Estimate	Actual time
To read a particular article in a magazine or newspaper		
To walk to the station or bus stop		
To write a letter to someone		
To mend something (a dress, a toy, the lawn mower)		

Many dyslexic people do not have a strong sense of time passing. How close was your estimate to the actual time? If it was less than the actual time, you need to be more realistic as to how much time you need to allow for many tasks.

Why don't I plan more things?
Because it is time-consuming and a bit boring and I feel 'lazy'.
Which probably means I find it hard!

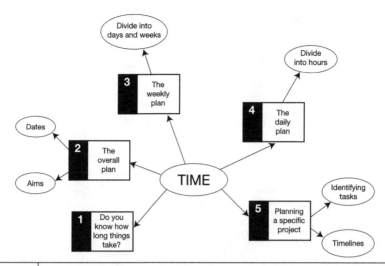

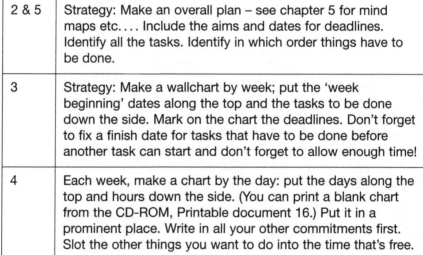

2 & 5	Strategy: Make an overall plan – see chapter 5 for mind maps etc.... Include the aims and dates for deadlines. Identify all the tasks. Identify in which order things have to be done.
3	Strategy: Make a wallchart by week; put the 'week beginning' dates along the top and the tasks to be done down the side. Mark on the chart the deadlines. Don't forget to fix a finish date for tasks that have to be done before another task can start and don't forget to allow enough time!
4	Each week, make a chart by the day: put the days along the top and hours down the side. (You can print a blank chart from the CD-ROM, Printable document 16.) Put it in a prominent place. Write in all your other commitments first. Slot the other things you want to do into the time that's free.

Figure 13 Using time to plan for important things

Try it for a week and see how it goes. See how it helps you.

Organising things you have to do

Paperwork is likely to be the most difficult thing to organise – it involves words and reading. Again planning is the key. And, if you keep your plan, you can use it for reference – 'where did I put that dry cleaner's receipt?'

Here is a plan for household information – set out as a mind map and also as a list:

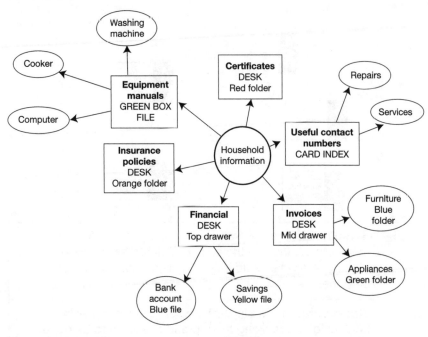

GREEN BOX FILE:
Equipment manuals
    computer
    cooker
    washing machine

CARD INDEX:
Useful contact numbers
    repairs
    services

DESK:
    Red folder: certificates
    Orange folder: insurance policies
    Middle drawer: invoices
    Blue folder: furniture
    Green folder: appliances
    Top drawer: financial
    Yellow file: savings
    Blue file: bank account

Figure 14 Household information

Strategies for organising time and things you have to do

Breaking down what you need to do and coming up with ideas for each step helps with organisation. Here are some ideas that have worked for others – some may be useful for you. Adapt them as you want. Highlight the useful ones and add a few of your own.

- For planning: mind maps (see chapter 5 and the CD-ROM in the

Writing section), lists, wallcharts – you can buy excellent ones that come with sticky stars and spots in different colours or design your own.

- For planning and remembering: Filofax, diary (the biggest you can carry around), electronic organisers, lists.

- For storing and organising paper: files of all kinds and in different colours: box files, Lever arch files, ring binders, folders and wallets, plastic wallets. Keep a supply of sticky labels for renaming used files.

- Put colour to good use – keep to the same colour for the same things, e.g. for all your financial things use yellow labels on files, use yellow files and document cases, yellow highlighters, yellow plastic pegs to keep things together, and so on.

- For time: set your watch, mobile phone, electronic organiser, timer, alarm clock, time management software, timeline (Gantt) charts, relations, friends and colleagues, allow extra time.

- For storing and organising information: card index, filing systems, the folder system on your computer, tape recorder.

- For prioritising: filing trays, review of previous lists.

- For coping with procedures: write instructions in your own words as you do things, or record on tape if you prefer.

- For organising objects and things: create a specific place.

ACTIVITY 14 – What do you need to organise?

This activity is a bit like making a New Year's resolution. We want you to identify something in your life that needs organising and then plan how to go about it.

First ask yourself what you want to organise.

It is worth spending some time on the things that really bug you.

Take a look at the things we have planned for below. Print out this table from the CD-ROM, Printable document 7. Add the one thing that you want to work better for you in the future. Think of some strategies that might work. You can use or adapt any of those we have suggested in this chapter but hopefully you may come up with something creative of your own.

What I want to organise	Strategies
I want to take all the right things with me to work each day	Stick **a list** to the front door. Put the standard items at the top and leave room for things you need occasionally **Collect everything** together by the door the night before
I want to get fit to run the marathon	**Make a plan:** type of exercise/ type of diet **Gather information:** costs of facilities, clothing, hours of opening of gym. **Make a chart:** identify the time required. Find space in your life. **Set up reminders:** timer on your watch or mobile phone. Post-it notes. **Make a chart:** to measure your progress.

My diary is a lifeline. I divide each page into two columns; one is for work lists, meetings etc., and the other one is for home time – yoga class, note for me to pick up someone at 7.00 etc. Every day I use the diary for work and I am then reminded of the other things to do later. I can also plan ahead, so when I think of something I can jot it into a day some weeks ahead.

Coping with a workload
Because things can take you much longer, make sure you:

- allow enough time;
- have a good plan;
- understand what is expected;
- don't waste time on non-essential things;
- don't go off at a tangent – stay focused;
- don't panic!

In this chapter we have encouraged you to think about:

- how you organise time and things you have to do;
- what it is that you want to organise;
- some useful ideas to adapt to suit you.

7

Handling numbers

Don't skip this chapter if you've always hated numbers, arithmetic and maths. There is something here for you. Everyone needs a little maths – in budgeting, travelling, cooking and DIY. Some of you may need a lot of maths – you may be a student studying science or technology. In this chapter we start by explaining the root of some of the difficulties. Later we give you a toolbox of strategies to try.

Many dyslexic people are very good at maths. They have an excellent understanding of the concepts but they may have difficulty with remembering the sequence of operations, times tables, or have difficulty with the language of maths in the same way as any other aspect of language. You may think you're no good at maths because you've been told so – but you may just take a more intuitive approach.

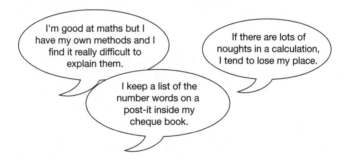

Dyscalculia (dis-cal-ku-lee-a)

You will hear the term dyscalculia mentioned. It is sometimes referred to as dyslexia with numbers. The difficulties are very similar to the problems that dyslexic people may have with words, but for some people they only seem to occur with numbers. We usually find that they may have overcome any word difficulties by using good strategies – leaving problems still with numbers.

Dyslexia and maths

If you are dyslexic it's likely that you took longer to learn mathematical symbols – which include the numbers themselves, as well as symbols such as + (addition) and x (multiplication).

Many difficulties can be due to memory: remembering which order to do things in, remembering formulas, remembering the meaning of mathematical words such as 'factorise', 'integrate', 'trigonometry' etc.

The table below compares the effects of dyslexia with words and numbers.

Area of difficulty	Effects on literacy (words)	Effects on numeracy (numbers)
Coding and decoding	Relating sounds to letters and letters to sounds	Relating numbers, letters and symbols to their meaning
	Difficulties distinguishing letters such as *b* and *d*	Difficulties distinguishing maths notation like *x* and *+*, *6 and 9*
Sequencing	Difficulties with the alphabet, months, letters in wrong order	Losing the place when going through a sequence of procedures, figures in wrong order
Memory	Difficulties with spelling	Difficulties with formulas, forgetting instructions. rote learning difficulties – times tables
Processing speed	Slow reading and writing words and numbers	
Lack of confidence	Anxiety over getting ideas down on paper	Anxiety over how to tackle the task
Words	Remembering subject-specific words	
Organisation	Unstructured essays and reports, untidy work	Setting out calculations in an unconventional way

In this chapter we use some of the strategies that you may already use with reading, writing and spelling to help you with numbers. Managing numbers is a bit like managing letters and words, i.e. many of the difficulties that you face with words may also arise with numbers. First we will look at mathematical learning styles and then at some of the characteristics of numbers and maths that cause people problems.

Mathematical learning styles

Do we all approach maths in the same way?
The answer to this is 'no'. There are two main types of learning styles in maths: the inchworm and the grass hopper (Steve Chinn).

The inchworm represents the type of person who learns in a stepwise way and who approaches any problem in much the same way, i.e. by deduction.

The grasshopper, on the other hand, tackles problems in an intuitive way, coming up with the answers but not necessarily able to explain how.

But in reality, the world isn't made up of inchworms and grasshoppers. We all tend to be a bit of both and will use one of the two approaches depending on the situation: hopefully, we choose the one that best suits us for the task in hand. If you are having difficulties with something mathematical, ask yourself whether you are acting like the inchworm or the grasshopper – and then try an approach that the other one would use. It just might help. The following activity will help you to discover whether you are predominantly an inchworm or a grasshopper.

✍ ACTIVITY 15 – Your predominant mathematical style

Answer either 'yes' or 'no' to the questions below. If your answer is 'sometimes', then decide what you prefer to do.

	Yes	No
1. Do you pay attention to detail?	▓	
2. Do you use formulas or recipes?	▓	
3. Do you do things in order?	▓	
4. Do you check your answers by going through the sum again?	▓	
5. Do you estimate calculations?		▓
6. Do you work back from your answer to check?		▓
7. Do you adjust numbers to make the calculation easier?		▓
8. Do you do some calculations in your head?		▓

If most of your answers are in the shaded boxes then you are probably an inchworm. If most of your answers are in the unshaded boxes, then you are probably a grasshopper. Perhaps you're a bit of both. Good mathematicians tend to use both approaches – choosing the right one suitable for the particular task. This activity has given you a chance to think about the way you do things generally. If you lean more towards one than the other, this may make life a bit difficult so try approaching some things the other way.

If you are predominantly a grasshopper, you may have been taught in a class of inchworms by a predominantly inchworm teacher. Being taught by inchworms can be bad news for dyslexic grasshoppers. Sometimes we don't or can't seem to set out the calculations in the way we are taught, but we still come up with the right answer. Our work may be marked as wrong or heavily corrected. This can lead to a loss of confidence and probably a dislike of maths.

Dyslexic-type problems and strengths

About 60 per cent of dyslexic people have some difficulties with maths, but these are not usually conceptual difficulties. They are to do with the *procedures* involved in solving the problem.

The difficulties can include:

- Decoding the numbers, letters and symbols.
- Remembering the procedures.
- Understanding and remembering the language of maths, science and technology.

Because many dyslexic people have a 'right-brained' learning style and see things holistically and intuitively, they may be very good at making connections and seeing patterns. So those who find ways to overcome the decoding and language difficulties are likely to enjoy and be good at maths.

Coding and decoding

When you look at numbers, letters and symbols your brain has to decide what they mean. This decoding is done in the working memory and is, for most people, a fast and automatic process. Dyslexia can affect dealing with numbers in two main ways:

- by slowing down the process;
- by causing errors due to forgetting numbers or mistaking say 6 for 9.

These kinds of difficulty are likely to affect arithmetic but not understanding. Many people who say that they're 'no good at maths' really mean that they have trouble with the arithmetic. And being slower to complete the arithmetic than other people doesn't mean you're less intelligent!

Numbers themselves are just codes for quantities. Symbols are codes for operations (see Figure 15 below). We know that many dyslexics have problems with coding and decoding – getting letters and groups of letters wrong. It's the same with numbers and maths symbols.

Procedures: rules and sequencing

We have to remember the rules of maths too. You probably find learning by rote almost impossible – such as learning the times tables. The key to learning rules is to understand them.

Most dyslexics have problems getting things in the right order – this can cause them to have difficulties with maths, including quite simple arithmetic. For example:

• Long division involves a sequence of steps. If one step is missed out or in the wrong order, then the answer will be wrong.
• Writing numbers down incorrectly – a dyslexic may not spot the difference between 1066, 1099, 1660 or 1990; they look very similar to someone who has sequencing difficulties.
• Problems getting the decimal point in the right place.

Language of maths
Just look at some of the ways we say the same thing in maths:

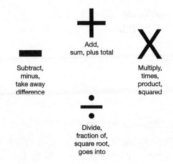

Figure 15

✍ ACTIVITY 16

There are other words that mean the same thing as the symbols in Figure 15. To which group do you think each of these words belongs?*

decrease, increase, and, less than, share, subtraction, division, power of, group, more than, split, addition, of

So we can see that dealing with numbers can be a source of difficulty. Just as in literacy, you can find imaginative and creative ways to help you cope. The rest of this chapter gives you some ideas to try – use them but, better still, adapt them or create your own to suit you.

---

* + increase, and, more than, addition; – decrease, less than, subtraction; x power of, of; ÷ split, group, share, division.

Your toolbox: number control!

Using your learning style
You can adapt the strategies in this toolbox to suit your own learning style. If you have strong visual skills, then use visual strategies. If you aren't technically minded then avoid technology until you have developed some confidence in it. But don't struggle with a strategy if it isn't working – try something else. There is more than one way to learn things. Make your learning multisensory: draw a diagram *and* listen to the words. Learn by doing something rather than just reading about it. Relax, make it fun.

This reference table gives suggestions for strategies to use – they are explained in detail on the following pages.

Your number needs	Suggested strategies: see Number section of the CD-ROM for some examples
Memory strategies Remembering standard procedures for doing calculations and manipulating numbers Mental arithmetic	Table squares Charts and diagrams Squared paper Calculator Mnemonics Your personal dictionary/glossary Estimation Cuisenaire rods

Your number needs	Suggested strategies: see Number section of the CD-ROM for some examples
Sequencing and directional strategies Remembering the order in which procedures are carried out. Remembering right and left.	Squared paper Model answers Verbalisation Personal checklist
Visual perceptual and spatial strategies Coping with symbols, confusable numbers, decimal points, powers etc., coping with graphs and tables.	Colour Squared paper Visual enhancement Tape recorder Cuisenaire rods
Language strategies Remembering the range of terms that mean the same, remembering labels, e.g. numerator/denominator.	Visualisation Your personal dictionary/glossary Colour Mnemonics Chunking Cuisenaire rods

Ideas and strategies
For examples of ideas and strategies, see the Number section of the CD-ROM.

Association
Link anything new that you learn to something you already know such as linking your bank PIN with a birthday. Don't forget that you can alter PINs to a number that is memorable for you – but not anything too obvious such as your own birthday! You can reset some combination locks to the number you want.

Calculator
Using a calculator helps to avoid errors with times tables and carrying figures over in sums. But it is possible to make a mistake keying in the numbers, so:

- Check that your answers are sensible by using the estimation strategy below.
- Do it slowly and twice to see if you get the same answer!
- Say the numbers and operations out loud as you key them in – this helps to avoid errors.

Avoid calculators with small keys. If yours are rather small, use a pen or small stick to press the keys.

Charts and diagrams
If you have good visual skills, you may find it easier to remember things if you use a chart or diagram. You may be able to use a ready-made one or you could devise your own. Here is a simple example to illustrate what we mean:

You might want to work out how much carpet to order, or how much paint to buy to decorate a wall. You need the *area*. This means you need to multiply the *length* by the *breadth* for the carpet, or the *length* by the *height* for the wall. You can use Figure 16 to help you remember that to work out the *area* of anything you take the two dimensions and multiply them.

Length

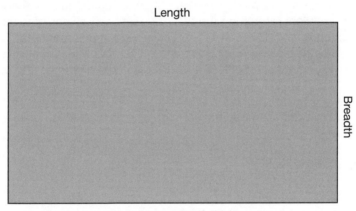

Area equals (=) *length* times (x) *breadth*

Figure 16

This is a basic example, but the idea can be used in quite complicated calculations too.

Chunking
If you need to remember a number the safest way is to write it down, saying it aloud as you write it, to make sure that you've written it correctly. But another way to remember is to 'chunk' it. Instead of remembering 11 digits for a telephone number, break it down: 039 08 274 066.

Concrete examples
It's very difficult, if not impossible, for you to learn something that you don't understand. Many people find it difficult to remember concepts

and theories that are abstract. Having concrete examples helps you to understand *and* remember. For example, you might find it difficult to remember the formula: 'the area of something is the length times the breadth' – see example above. But if you think of area as the amount of carpet you need and remember that you have to measure the length and breadth of the room, this helps you to remember the method.

Again this is a very simple example but it gives you an idea that you can apply to more complicated situations. Try to use real-life situations rather than abstract ideas – ones that relate to things in which you are interested.

Cuisenaire rods
Doing things physically is a great aid to understanding and remembering. Cuisenaire rods are small coloured sticks that have a different colour for each length – you may have used them at school. They are excellent for getting the feel of quantity. They can also be added together and taken away physically. Addition, subtraction, multiplication and division are good examples of abstract concepts. With the rods, you can lay out different lengths and see how they add up.

Estimation
After you have done your sums, you can ask yourself if you have a sensible answer.

Here is a simple example:

Sam had £324.24 in her account. She wrote a cheque for £299.72. She did a written calculation to see how much money she had left. She had problems subtracting and her answer came out at £172.52. If she had done an estimate, she could have said that the cheque was about £300 and then realised that she only had about £25 left.

Personal specialist dictionary or glossary
Make yourself a specialist 'dictionary' either in a small notebook or on index cards. Whenever you meet a new technical word, or one you can't remember, write it down. Underneath, write an explanation and the sentence, phrase or formula where you first came across it. You might add associated words, a diagram or sketch and the relevant mathematical symbol (π, % or $\sqrt{\ }$, for example). Use colour to make it memorable. Arrange your dictionary in the way that suits you best. It doesn't have to be in alphabetical order – you could do it in topic order.

Mnemonics
Mnemonics are memory aids usually using initials or word associations. For example,

denominator-downstairs.

You could also use some of the ideas for mnemonics in chapter 8.

Model answers
If you are studying a maths-based subject, ask your tutor for some model answers of typical problems. There is a limited number of ways to solve problems. A selection of model answers will give you confidence that you are going along the right lines or they may help to get you started.

Personal checklist
If you regularly make the same mistakes, it is worth making your own personal checklist. You could add these to a standard checklist, or combine them with a spelling checklist that includes your own common errors. If it isn't too long, your list could go on a length of card to use as a bookmark.

Personalised ready reckoner
In your work or studies you may have to use the same processes regularly. To save looking these up, have your own ready reckoner for things you often need. For example, you could have a list of approximate values:

- 80km ~ 50 miles
- 1″ ~ 2½ cm

Squared paper
Squared paper helps with 'place value' – keeping your calculations in lines and columns so that the 'units', 'tens' etc. appear in the same columns. You are much less likely to lose figures and your work will look neat. It also helps to form symbols by giving you a square in which to draw them.

Times table square
Multiplication tables can be difficult or impossible for dyslexic people to learn by rote in the conventional way. You can carry a folded table square in your bag or pocket for reference. If you want to know what 7 x 8 is, then look along the 7th row to where it crosses the 8th column and you have the answer – 56! You can print this square from the CD-ROM, Printable document 9.

0	1	2	3	4	5	6	7	8	9	10	11	12
1	1	2	3	4	5	6	7	8	9	10	11	12
2	2	4	6	8	10	12	14	16	18	20	22	24
3	3	6	9	12	15	18	21	24	27	30	33	36
4	4	8	12	16	20	24	28	32	36	40	44	48
5	5	10	15	20	25	30	35	40	45	50	55	60
6	6	12	18	24	30	36	42	48	54	60	66	72
7	7	14	21	28	35	42	49	56	63	70	77	84
8	8	16	24	32	40	48	56	64	72	80	88	96
9	9	18	27	36	45	54	63	72	81	90	99	108
10	10	20	30	40	50	60	70	80	90	100	110	120
11	11	22	33	44	55	66	77	88	99	110	121	132
12	12	24	36	48	60	72	84	96	108	120	132	144

 When you see the times tables set out like this, you can begin to see patterns. There's more about this on the CD-ROM in the Numbers section.

Gypsy method of multiplying
You can use this method only for numbers from 6 to 10 – you have to be able to multiply numbers below 6 in your head or in some other way.

Number the fingers and thumbs on both hands from 6 to 10, starting with the thumbs. You can do this with a ballpoint pen. Place your palms together but not touching.

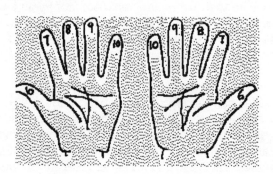

Figure 17

Example: to multiply 8 by 9.

- Put the tip of the finger marked 8 of one hand to touch the tip of the finger marked 9 on the other hand.
- Count the fingers and thumbs from your thumbs up to and including the two fingers that are touching – 7. This is the number of tens – 70.
- Count the remaining fingers on one hand and multiply it by the number of remaining fingers on the other – two fingers left on one hand and one on the other: 2 x 1 = 2. These are the units.
- Put the tens and units together for the correct answer: 72.

It may seem a bit confusing and you'll need a lot of practice, but it can really work. It's a useful way of checking those awkward tables above 5 times that seem to give the most trouble.

Tape recorder
- A tape recorder can help with checking: it's often better to find your own errors as it can help with learning but they can be difficult to spot. Ask someone to read your calculations onto tape – words, figures and symbols. You can then listen to see if it is what you meant to write. You may have put ÷ when you meant x.
- You can practise reciting times tables – if you still feel you want to learn them.

Verbalisation
This means saying things aloud, or 'hearing' the sound in your head if you are in a place where you can't or don't want to be heard.

- Say it out loud, tracking each figure with your finger as you go. Using your visual and auditory senses, and to some extent your touch as well, can straighten out numbers that bewilder the eye alone: 1066, for example, is easily confused with 1099, 1660, 1990, 6601.
- Say the words for symbols aloud. It helps to remember them.
- Chanting chunks (see chunking ideas above) to a familiar tune or a rhythm can help. Tunes such as the 'Can-Can' are surprisingly adaptable!
- If you are a student and need to remember equations and formulae, try saying them in words:

$F = ma$
This is the formula – **Force** *equals* **mass** of the object *times* its **acceleration**.
So, remember the words if you find it difficult to remember the formula. But, note, the best thing about formulas is that you don't have to remember the spelling!!

Visual enhancement
- Makes easily confusable numbers such as 6 and 9 different in some way.
- Makes symbols memorable in a visual way:
  < means 'less than' and looks like a slightly tilted '**L**' standing for **L**ess than.
- Enlarge the decimal point: 342•10.
- You can use <u>colour</u> in number work as well as with words. For example, you can group maths words together that have the same meaning using the same colour. Taking the example in Figure 15, each of the four sets of words and symbols would be a different colour (see Number section on the CD-ROM). This will help you to remember which ones are closely linked.

Visualisation
- See in your mind's eye a picture that reminds you of the word: you could visualise 'ellipse' with the double L inside an ellipse, for example:

This will help you to remember how to spell it even though people will know what you mean if you spell it with only one L. Technical words are often misspelled by non-dyslexic people too!

- Remember three-dimensional shapes by linking them with a familiar object: a sphere looks like an orange; a cylinder is like a beer can.
- Making numbers larger can help.

Postscript
It seems to be OK to admit to 'being no good at maths', more so than admitting that you have writing or spelling difficulties. Most dyslexic difficulties create errors in decoding and doing things in the right order. Many dyslexic people have the ability to understand mathematical concepts and have outstanding creative and spatial abilities.

I have absolutely no problems understanding quite difficult maths: algebra, vectors, calculus. But I used to make stupid mistakes in calculations because my work was so messy and I lost marks. Now, at work I do everything using Excel, Mathcad or on squared paper and this stops me making a lot of those silly errors.

In this chapter we have looked at:

- mathematical learning styles: inchworm and grasshopper;
- the type of difficulties dyslexic people have with numbers;
- some ideas and strategies for handling numbers.

8

Making memory work for you

'Remember remember the fifth of November ...'

Because of this rhyme, most people can remember that Guy Fawkes tried to blow up Parliament on November 5th. But it doesn't help them to remember which year!

In this chapter we will look at memory – how it works and how you can make it work to your advantage.

Short- and long-term memory

Short-term memory
Short-term memory, often called 'the working memory', really is short term, so some things are processed almost without you being aware. The brain handles small chunks of information and puts them together for a purpose.

For example, when you read the sentence

You must cross the road to go to the cinema

in order to understand the sentence you have to remember the beginning until you get to the end, so that you can put it all together and make sense of it. At the same time, your memory has to cope with decoding the letters into sounds, putting them together to make words and identifying the words.

Similarly when doing a mental calculation, you have to remember the original part while you are working out the calculation. For example if you are calculating 100 minus 88, you have to keep remembering the 100 and the 88, take 8 from 0 which means remembering to borrow 1, then take 9 from 10 and remember that you already have two units. The answer is 12.

It's amazing how our working memory copes! However, once the sentence is understood, or the answer calculated, we usually forget the original bits of information – the words or the numbers.

Long-term memory
This is the memory we are usually referring to when we talk about 'memory'. It represents information that is stored for long periods of time. Remembering your name, where you went to primary school, where you went on holiday last year – all need your long-term memory.

On the whole, long-term memory covers everything from something you experienced two minutes ago, two days ago or 20 years ago.

'I know I put it in a safe place!'

There are two types of long-term memory:

• Episodic – remembering a particular incident such as a visit to the cinema last week.

- Semantic – remembering the meaning of a word or the name of a particular object.

Remembering is not forgetting
What about forgetting?

- We forget most of what we see, hear or experience within a few seconds! Some pieces of information stick in our minds for much longer.
- Interruptions are really bad news, particularly for dyslexic people. If you are interrupted you will probably lose a substantial part of what you are trying to remember. The thread is broken – it's gone!
- 'Use it or lose it'. For example: a group who took part in a resuscitation course could only recall 15 per cent of it after 12 months because they hadn't used their new skills.

> Why don't I forget how to ride a bike after 20 years?

The actions have become automatic – one action cues the next.

Remembering is about being able to get to the information
Getting at the information we've stored away is called *recall* or *retrieval*. All the ideas that we introduce in this chapter will help you to store the information in your brain so that it can be recalled or retrieved when you need it. How often have you said 'it's on the tip of my tongue' or 'I know I saw it in the middle of a page'? These are 'cues' but they are not strong enough to retrieve the information. We usually need more than one cue or association for efficient recall.

Each time you recall something, the pathways in your brain that access the information become easier. It's like the footpath across a field of fully grown corn. It's hard work for the first person to hack their way across it – but once three or four people have walked that way, the path is easier and clearer. So go over things several times that you want to remember.

Check them out regularly. Use them. Keep the pathways in your brain open.

What helps you to remember?

Here is a list of possible things you might want to remember and some suggestions to help.

Thing to remember	How you might do it	Type of strategy
Names	Imagine the face with the name written below it on a billboard	Visual
Phrases for using in a foreign country	Imagine yourself in various situations in which you have to use these phrases – use them.	Doing/acting
Numbers	Group them rhythmically: grouping in threes works best as it seems to reduce the tendency to recall them in the wrong order	Auditory
	Speak them aloud – don't just read them to yourself: articulating and hearing the sounds of the numbers registers them in your auditory as well as your visual short-term memory	Auditory/visual
Where you left something: a spatial orientation problem such as finding a car in a car park	Find landmarks to link to – such as the flint church nearby	Visual

✍ ACTIVITY 17 – How do *you* remember?

Look at the following and think about how you might remember them. What techniques do you use? Look at the strategies you used and decide whether each was visual (seeing), auditory (hearing) or kinaesthetic (doing, touching), or a combination of two or more (as we have done above).

Thing to remember	How you do it	Type of strategy?
The cashpoint PIN		
The route to somewhere you don't go very often		
Where you put your photo albums		
Important information for something you have to write		

You probably used several different techniques – you used strategies.

- Maybe you saw the number in your mind; perhaps you wrote it down on your hand and then copied it onto a piece of paper.
- For the route – you might have visualised it in your mind or imagined a map. You might have drawn it using symbols for distinctive landmarks such as the church on the corner.
- You may keep all your photograph albums on one easy-to-reach shelf in the living room or know where they are because they are bright red.
- You may remember information you need by putting it all in one place, perhaps in a file marked with the title so you can find it easily.

Remembering is all about using strategies. But before you look at further strategies you might try identifying the different kinds of things you want to remember.

*I was at a concert. The violin soloist was wonderful and I really wanted to remember her name: Elizabeth Wallfisch. So I imagined the Queen (**Elizabeth**) sitting on a **wall**, dangling her feet over a painted **fish** on the wall. Later I couldn't remember her name but I remembered the picture that I had invented. I worked back to her name.*

Improving your memory

Encoding

We're going to use the word 'encoding' a lot. It is a useful technical word and it means the way we get our brains to interact with the information in our short-term memory so that we can store it in our long-term memory.

When we talk about how to 'improve' memory, we are usually talking about **encoding** more efficiently so that we get something into our long-term memory and improve the way we retrieve it. We are imprinting it in our brain in such a way that our brain can recognise it when we want to access it.

It's a myth that memory gets worse with age. With the exception of some medical conditions, the problem is just that older people have more stored information that takes time to find. Our memories do seem to fill up as the years pass, adding vast numbers of experiences. Imagine more and more things piled untidily in a heap – like a pile of unsorted washing – and you can see that it can get harder and harder to 'sort' and 'retrieve' as the pile grows. If you sort by colour, for example into separate piles, it will be quicker to find a particular garment. The same is true in your memory. If you store things away by linking them to something already memorable, it will be easier to retrieve that fact or memory.

> *The person who thinks over his experiences most and weaves them into systematic relations with each other will be the one with the best memory* (William James, psychologist and philosopher).

You really can improve your memory – this means improving the way you store and retrieve information. It is not as if you are actually 'losing' things – it is more a case that you cannot find where you put them.

Here are 13 suggestions – the 13 Ms to make things more retrievable:

You need to:

- Make sense of it – it's very hard to remember something you don't understand.
- Make it stick* – we remember things in which we are interested.
- Make it memorable* – we remember things that are unusual or exaggerated.
- Make it multisensory* – see it, touch it, hear it, do it, smell it.

- Make use of your memory style – bright colours, rhyming words, acting it out (refer back to the learning style activity in chapter 3).
- Make it organised* – into groups, patterns, categories.
- Make it into chunks* – a few things at a time, 5–9 chunks work best.
- Make time for review – without reviewing what we have learned we forget 80% after 24 hours.
- Make a mnemonic* – build links to things you can remember.
- Make a mind map.
- Make the best time and place for memory work.*
- Make links – to things you already understand.*
- Make time to practise – recalling improves the retrieval pathways.

Now let's look at some of these suggestions (those marked *) in some more detail.

Making it stick
A TV advertisement was shown recently more than a 1000 times but, despite this, it became clear that it hadn't stuck in people's minds. It did not catch people's attention nor did it prompt them to act on it. Nothing gets stored in your long-term memory unless you do something to get it there.

You have to:

PAY ATTENTION *and*	
Pay attention: Sit up, get ready for action, be aware of what needs doing, concentrate, clear the mind of other things	**Process actively:** Use your strengths, make links, make it multisensory, apply some of the 13 Ms

Try this:

When you meet a person for the first time you usually concentrate on making appropriate remarks. You probably don't repeat the name three times which would give you some chance of remembering it the next time you meet. Try repeating their name as they say it: say 'Hello, Jim'. Then, during the conversation with Jim include his name several times: 'Do you live near here, Jim?' 'Jim, what do you think of . . .' etc.

It also helps to link the person's name with some visual characteristic. For example, if Jim has reddish hair you can say to yourself (and so store in your memory) 'red Jim'.

You are PAYING ATTENTION: Listening for Jim's name, looking for visual characteristics

and PROCESSING ACTIVELY: Using his name several times, linking his name to his hair colour

Making it memorable
Here are some ideas to make things memorable:

Exaggerate the size, the shape and the sound of whatever you are trying to remember. Imagine it as massive – write it out in huge letters. Make something more colourful.

Making it multisensory
When you are trying to remember something important, make it multisensory, a strategy we have mentioned several times in previous chapters. We remember something even better when we use more than one of our senses. This is called *enriched* encoding, i.e. we are using more routes in our brain to recall something.

Stop for a minute and remember, for example, your first day at the seaside. You may not now easily recall where or when it was, but you might well be able to remember:

- the smell of the sea;
- the feel of the sand through your toes;
- the sight of the waves with their breakers;
- the sound of seagulls;
- even the taste of a piece of seaside rock with the letters running through it.

All your senses were involved and that makes for a richly encoded memory. Any one aspect repeated later – such as the smell of the sea – can trigger all the others. Visit a rubbish disposal site and you may well be reminded of the sea. Why? Well, gulls tend to hang around inland waste disposal sites and their cries will trigger memories of the seaside.

The more ways the whole experience is encoded, the more your memory will be triggered, helping you to remember and recall things. We call this multisensory learning – learning using many senses.

Pause

Have you done Activity 4 from chapter 3 – the one that helps you to identify your preferred way of doing things? If not, then try it now.

- You may be more visual. Some people can imagine the actual book and where the information lies on the page.
- You may be better with sounds – you remember all sorts of television jingles, rhymes etc.
- You may remember something more easily when it is put into an interesting story or if you have personal experience of doing it.

Here are some ideas and strategies to match your learning style. Where possible, combine more than one idea from each section to make it multisensory.

Using visual memory – working through seeing
Use colour – highlight words, colour it in
Draw it – make an attractive poster, diagram, spider diagram or mind map
Adapt a diagram from a book and make it colourful
Use post-it notes in different colours and stick them up in prominent places
Try memory videos – details in the Memory section of the CD-ROM.

Using auditory memory – working through hearing
Put information onto audiotape and play it back several times ... while washing up, driving or relaxing
Repeat things aloud to yourself as if you were explaining it to someone
Discuss it with someone
Work with music in the background – *experiment with different kinds of music*

Using kinaesthetic memory – working through doing, touching, smelling
Act it out – make a story
Interact with the information – *ask questions, make notes, diagrams or drawings*
Put the information on index cards that you can pull out of your pocket every time you have a spare moment
Walk about while learning
Take regular breaks and do something physical
Try things out or imagine doing them

Making it organised

Put information you regularly confuse into categories that emphasise the differences and make it distinctive.

Think of it like holding six new-laid eggs in one hand. Now imagine holding an egg box filled with eggs. Which is easier to grasp? The same principle applies to your memory. Try focusing on the structure (the egg box) of what you want to remember, rather than the detail (the eggs). Groups of ideas are easier to encode and recall.

Our memory is a bit like a library. A disorganised memory would be like a library where all the books have just been placed on the shelves in any old order. Libraries arrange books in subject order and then in alphabetical order of the author's surname. This makes it easier to find a book.

The same thing applies to your memory.

When you learn, you decide how to organise the information and decide where to put it. This is the learning process.

Organising things you need to learn gives a structure and pattern to them and makes them easier to recall.

Make it into chunks

Your short-term memory can handle information and get it into your long-term memory better if what you are trying to learn is broken down into manageable chunks. Chunking is an excellent strategy for dyslexics. Here are some ways to chunk things:

- Chop long words into smaller words or syllables to learn the spelling.
- Pick out key words and just try to remember those.
- Separate things out visually – use space.
- Don't spend too long on any learning task without taking breaks.

Making a mnemonic

Any method, often a rhyme, which helps you to remember is called a mnemonic.

In fourteen hundred and ninety-two
Columbus sailed the ocean blue (and discovered America).

You have probably seen entertainers who perform amazing feats of memory with seemingly impossible sequences of cards, dates and telephone directories. They use mnemonics. The variation likely to suit most dyslexic people is called 'location mnemonics' because it uses seeing and doing strategies. Another, called the number-rhyme system, is described in the Memory section of the CD-ROM and would suit those who are better at remembering words and sounds.

Location mnemonics

First choose a location that is very familiar to you such as your home and garden, or the town where you live. Walk around your chosen area regularly in the same sequence, whether or not you have something to learn. Look carefully at it all – imprint it on your memory. Try imagining it with your eyes shut until you 'see' it just as if you were there.

Now look at whatever it is you need to remember. 'Walk' through your location in your mind using the route you always take and link everything you need to remember to things on your route. You can make it even more vivid by weaving a story. Then, all you have to do is walk around, or imagine, your route and the things you want to remember will pop into your mind.

It works because you can remember the route better than unconnected or loosely connected facts.

It's also very similar to making memory videos.

✍ ACTIVITY 18

Try to learn something that would be useful for you to be able to remember using location mnemonics:

1. Write down the facts you have to remember.
2. Choose your location. Walk round your location several times and commit it to memory.
3. Check your location in your mind.
4. Now walk round the location in your mind and link all the things you need to remember – one or two for each part of the location. Weave a story or see the facts as part of the location.
5. Next day, walk round your location – in reality or in your imagination – and try to remember the things in each place as you walk. Write them down as you recall them.
6. Check the list.

Making the best time and place for memory work
Time
There are certain times and places that are better for memorising things.

- Some people are better in the mornings, others later in the day. Experiment with different times to find which is best for you.
- There is evidence to suggest that we remember things we learn or do just before going to bed. On the other hand, we don't take anything in very well if we are tired. There is a balance to be struck here! If you relax after a hard day's work and then do some learning before going to sleep there is less interference from other things and the physiological process of consolidating the memory system in the brain during the night may help.
- How alert we are varies considerably. We don't learn so well if we are upset, concerned or in a state of panic.

Try out different times of the day and see if these ideas work for you.

Place
Find a good place to work in. Avoid distractions, especially visual ones. Background music of the right kind can be helpful in filtering out sudden distracting sounds. Remember you need a comfortable temperature, a comfortable seating position and good light.

Making links
Repetition is so often praised as the best way to learn something but it doesn't really work for complex information – for this we need to make links to things we already know. We can't remember complex

information by rote because we need to understand it. We then need to link it to something else which is firmly anchored in our memory.

It's like a series of boats all moored together with their ropes to the dock of our memory. You are relating new material as closely and as richly as you can to your own interests and previous knowledge.

Pause

Research has shown that commitment and enthusiasm are the most important aspects of the ability to remember and recall things. A schoolboy will remember all the names of his football heroes. So put some enthusiasm into what you are doing. Set yourself short-term aims – break the task into smaller ones and reward yourself in some way for achieving each. If you were trying to help someone else to remember and learn, you would reward and praise at each stage, almost without thinking. So do it for yourself too!

We will go out to supper on Friday after I have done this work.

Remembering to do regular things
For things that are **regular** you may need to think about different kinds of reminders that work for you. Ask yourself: *Does this task or activity come up regularly? Daily, weekly, monthly, annually?*

Much of this is concerned with good organisational strategies (see chapter 6) and remembering to check them. The simpler your system, the more likely you are to remember to check it. Electronic systems can be set up to remind you. For paper systems, such as wallcharts and diaries, you should build your checking into part of your routine: for example, you could always check your wall planner when you make your early morning cup of tea.

Improving memory by diet, supplements and exercise

Memory is definitely improved when our general health is good, so eat a balanced diet and take regular exercise. A balanced diet means plenty of fresh fruit and vegetables, a reasonable amount of protein, not too much starchy food, very little sugar and salt. Avoid fast foods which are generally too fatty. Keep within the guidelines on alcohol as too much can have a detrimental effect on memory. There is some evidence that fish oils help in brain functioning, so eat plenty of oily fish such as herring, sardines etc.

Before you spend too much time and money investigating supplements, check for food intolerance generally. People can develop an intolerance or allergy to many foods. Dairy produce and wheat are two of the most common. The effects can include tiredness, lack of concentration, headaches etc.

There is a big industry in alternative medicines and supplements: some claims are backed by scientific research, some are based on ancient medical practice and some are questionable. You may come across the following supplements:

- Omega3 – if your diet doesn't include enough fish oil.
- Algal DHA – for those who can't eat fish oil.
- Gingko and ginseng – ancient remedies.

More information can be found on the Internet.

Our advice is to try things sensibly:

- in the first instance try to improve your diet in order to gain the same benefits;

- check with your doctor if you are on other medications;
- take one product at a time over about three months and see if you notice any difference.

There is a definite relationship between exercise and learning – it really pays to take a break from brain work. A brisk 10-minute walk round the block or up and down the stairs will get you working more effectively than a quick sugar snack, because exercise releases endorphins in the brain. You will then be more alert and your memory will work better too.

Many people have found that Brain Gym® helps with memory and learning. It offers particular activities and movement sequences to improve your learning ability. You can find more information from their website (www.braingym.org). If you think it might help you, give it a try. Ask around – you may find someone who has experience of it. It is used a lot with children although it does also seem to work for many adults.

What do *you* need to remember?

✍ ACTIVITY 19 – What do you need to remember?

Jot down the main things you would like to be able to remember better.

You may find that they fall into different groups. You may have a list of 'facts' such as names, numbers, locations of objects, and a different list of more complicated ideas – notes for a report etc.

What strategies will you try? Jot down a list of any ideas in this chapter that you would like to try or any ideas that have been triggered in your mind by reading this. Keep the list in a safe place ready for when you next need to remember something.

In this chapter we have looked at:

- short- and long-term memory;
- how we best remember things;
- how you can improve memory and recall;
- a range of ideas and strategies to help you to remember things.

Quick tips for improving your memory:

- Make it interesting.
- Make it memorable.

Part 3
Resources for You

In this part there are two chapters and four appendices that give details of resources that you might find useful. There is a good spread of low, medium and high-tech resources.

Chapter 9:   Helping yourself with technology
               Hardware and software packages

Chapter 10: Looking wider
               Support from family and friends, alternative ideas and
               therapies, counselling

Appendices A Checklist for dyslexia
                B Useful and interesting books
                C Useful addresses
                D Glossary

9

Helping yourself with technology

There is no doubt that most dyslexic adults find that computers give them a huge amount of independence. Technical solutions of all kinds can help with reading, writing, spelling, grammar and organisation. In this chapter you can find medium and high tech ideas to help you.

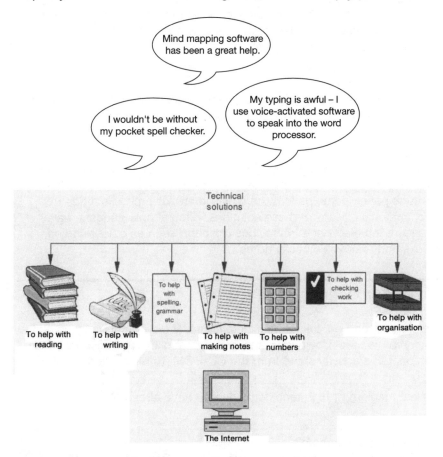

Figure 18 Finding your way around this chapter

We hope you will find this chapter informative even if you are wary of technology. It summarises the resources that are currently available in a non-technical way (prices quoted are approximate at the time of going to press). We hope it will help you to think about what would be useful.

Coping with new technology may be more difficult as you get older. Young people seem to cope as if they were born sending text messages or using computers. So give yourself time. It isn't easy to break a computer.

Technical solutions

We have grouped technical solutions as follows:

⌨ High tech
This relates to the technology developed at the latter part of the 20th century and includes sophisticated designs and materials, microprocessors, computers etc.

⌨ Medium tech
This includes items that use the technology developed during the early to mid 20th century such as recordings and photocopying.

🗀 Low tech
This is not discussed here but there is a list of useful items at the end of this chapter. It includes items that have been around for at least the last century: paper, pens, pencils, card, wood etc. or products made from such materials. Many of these solutions, often simple gadgets, have already been discussed in previous chapters such as colour coding, charts and removable sticky notes.

✍ ACTIVITY 20

Before you read on, take a minute to consider how technology could be useful for you. Jot down your answers to the following questions. You can print this activity sheet from the CD-ROM, Printable document 20.

What medium or high tech items do you have already?			
How do you use them? To their full advantage	Quite well	Basically	Not at all

Whether or not you have the technology, imagine that there is technology available for every situation. List three dyslexic difficulties that you would like a technical remedy for.
1
2
3

Now read on. We'll come back to this exercise later.

Technology to help with reading
Medium tech
Talking books
A lot of books are now available as recordings through the library or in bookshops. People like to listen to them while they are driving. If you want to read a book for pleasure, this may be a good option for you. Note, though, that most are abridged (edited to cut down their length), so you won't hear the full text.

> One student said: *I'm doing an Open University course. Most of their course books are on tape. This cuts down the amount I have to read.*

Coloured light
If you have found coloured overlays helpful (see chapter 4 and the Reading section of the CD-ROM), you may like to use a lamp with a coloured bulb. There is an excellent lamp (Optim-eyes) available that allows you to change the colour through the whole spectrum to suit you and the conditions (£260).

High tech – Computers and software
Using the standard software
Many documents at work or at college may be available as electronic files. With a computer you can adapt and use them to overcome some of your own dyslexic difficulties.

You can:

- Change the typeface and the size of the letters. Some people also find that double-line spacing makes text much easier to read.
- Change the colour of the letters and of the background.
- Alter the colours and fonts you see on your screen.

- Copy extracts from the text.
- Add your own notes to the text.

So it's worth asking whether you can have the document on a disk to use on your own computer.

Speech output – text reader – text to speech
These are all terms used for the same thing. With appropriate software, your computer can read the text out loud as it appears on the screen. You need a multi-media computer for this, or you might be able to upgrade an older model. The synthesised speech may not be easy to listen to, but these artificial voices are improving all the time.

Speech output can be useful in the same way as recordings and talking books. It helps:

- comprehension and concentration
- pronunciation of new and unfamiliar words
- skim reading
- proof-reading your own work.

Take time to consider which package is best for you – some are definitely not useful for dyslexic people. Check the following. Does it:

- highlight the word as it reads it?
- allow automatic read back by word, sentence or paragraph?
- offer alternatives in case you've got it wrong?

Costs vary, but the range is approximately £140–£260. Specialist advice is essential (see appendix C).

Reading pen
A reading pen is a miniature scanner about the size of a chunky pen. It has a synthesised voice and can be used with an ear-piece. It reads out individual words and can give their definitions, although it might not recognise some highly specialised words. Prices are still quite high (£170), but are coming down. There are similar devices for scanning small extracts of text – e.g. quotations and things you want to remember – so that you can load them into your computer.

Scanners
If you want to read something by listening to it, and it isn't available as a recording or an electronic file, a scanner might be worth having. It's a hand-held or flat-bed device (something like a photocopier) that copies

the text and converts it to a word-processed document. You can then adapt and use that in all the ways we've already suggested. The software that converts the image to text sometimes has problems when presented with unclear print, symbols or complex layouts. However, such packages are getting more sophisticated and some can even read handwriting. Cost – £50 upwards.

Technology to help with writing – getting the ideas down

Many dyslexic people are articulate and express themselves well verbally. Slow writing, lack of confidence with spelling or grammar and other difficulties can interfere with the flow of ideas. Technology can help by separating the 'transcription' skills from the 'composition' – the creative ideas and structure (as described in chapter 5).

🖳 Medium tech

Tape or digital recorders
Dictating can remove many of the difficulties of 'transcription' (see chapter 5). You can dictate your ideas into an audio-cassette recorder, play it back and type the ideas into your word processor like an audio-typist. You can use your word processor to correct and edit your text. Cost: very cheap to £170+ for a sophisticated digital recorder.

Coloured light
See under the reading section above.

🖥 High tech – Computers and software

Standard word processors
Set up your word processor so that your text is as easy as possible for you to read. Ensure your screen is free from reflections and adjust its brightness and contrast. Some choices you can make within standard word processor packages are:

- The colour of the text and the background.
- The shape and size of the letters. You can also use the zoom facility to display the 'page' on your screen in your preferred size.
- Make your text left-justified (as in this book). Many dyslexic people find that this helps to overcome some visual distortion.
- Set up AutoCorrect to correct errors you're particularly likely to make, and to complete words and phrases you type in frequently.
- Add commonly used commands to the toolbar to avoid hunting through menus.
- Use Outline mode to see the structure of your document and change it easily.

- Create a template if you're going to produce several documents of a similar kind.
- Be sure to save your work frequently – at least every five minutes.

If you want to find out more about these facilities, use the Help menu. You might want to look for an IT course at your local college. They are often inexpensive and sometimes free.

Touch typing
It is very useful to be able to touch type – to know which fingers hit which keys so that you can type without looking at the keyboard. We recommend that you should try to learn this skill as the brain doesn't have to think about the letters as you type – it becomes automatic. It may help also with spelling. There are a number of software packages for learning to type (£20–£50).

Voice-recognition software
Packages that fall in this group allow you to talk directly to your computer, which then transcribes your speech into word-processed text. You may have trouble if your speech isn't particularly clear or varies a lot. You'll need training and so will your computer – it has to learn to recognise *your* voice. This may mean several hours of work. You'll probably need to weigh up the inconveniences of the software against the degree of difficulty you have with the keyboard. Many voice-recognition software packages are available at affordable prices (£50–£500). Seek advice from a specialist and buy the best you can afford. Before you buy anything, try it out.

Technology to help with words – spelling, grammar etc.
You might want to check a spelling or the meaning of a word, or find the right word to use. Difficulties with reading and alphabetic order can make using a dictionary hard work, if not impossible. Technology can help.

⌨ Medium tech
Spelling
There are a number of hand-held spell checkers available (£30–£50). Some include definitions (as in a dictionary) and some include a thesaurus that will offer you alternative words you can use. See the general discussion about using spell checkers on computers below. It is much quicker to use these electronic devices than paper-based ones and they are more portable than a computer. But don't get anything too small because it will be difficult to read. If you are a student and intend buying a small, portable spell checker to use in exams, make sure that the one you choose will be permitted.

🖥 High tech – Computers and software
Spelling and grammar checkers
Standard word processors offer some help with spelling and grammar. Some packages provide help with words that are spelt differently but sound the same ('hear' and 'here') by giving you an idea of the meaning. Some use grammar rules to help you decide on the right word.

Some software will highlight or even correct mistakes as you type. If you find that these interruptions interfere with the flow of your ideas, you can alter the default settings so that the checks are not made automatically. You can run the check when you are ready. Make sure that your language setting is correct: UK English for most English-speaking countries, US English for North America. The default setting is often US English – change the setting to the one you need.

Spell checkers are useful but they can't be relied on completely. They cannot distinguish a misspelled word if the misspelling is itself a word. If you mistype 'boat' as 'beat' or if you type 'their' instead of 'there', the spell checker will not recognise an error has been made as the mistyped word is also a real word. More advanced packages will pick up some of these and ask which word you mean. If you're concerned about spelling, consider purchasing speech output software as well – see above.

You can run the grammar checker when you have finished. Bear in mind that some of its comments are not particularly helpful. One grammar checker, for example, questions whether you should be using 'that' instead of 'which'. If you type

They was going out

it will query the subject–verb agreement. The word 'was' will be highlighted and it will suggest using 'were'. This can be very useful if your grammar is a bit wobbly.

Predictive software
Predictive software is a package that offers you a choice of words. Some other packages also include a predictive facility. When you type the first few letters of a word, a list of the words you use most commonly will be displayed. Click on the one you want and it will be inserted for you. For example, if you type 'psy' you might get this list:

psychology
psychologist

> psyche
> psychiatry
> psychoanalyst
> psychotic

The more letters you can type in, the more likely the word you want will be included in the selection. The software remembers how often and how recently you've used the words it comes up with and lists the most likely ones at the top.

Meaning
Good dictionaries are available on CD-ROMs. If you type a word or highlight it in the text you're reading or writing, you can use the dictionary to give you the full definition or, if you have sound, to check the pronunciation.

Finding the right word or another word
A thesaurus is a dictionary of synonyms – words or phrases that have the same or similar meaning. It is useful for finding a more appropriate word or finding an alternative when you have used a particular word too often. A thesaurus will help you to increase your vocabulary and improve the quality of your written work. Some word processors include one, but, like dictionaries, it is possible to buy an excellent thesaurus on CD-ROM.

Technology to help with making notes
Making notes usually means doing several tasks at the same time – listening or reading, understanding, summarising, writing. This can be difficult if you're dyslexic, but technology can help.

⌨ Medium tech
Recorders
Cassette recorders, mini-disk and digital recorders are all ways of recording sound. Recorders have improved with the advances in technology so buy the best you can afford. You can do a lot with the basic cassette recorder that has been around since the 1960s, but digital recorders have many additional facilities. You can edit the recording and they provide many hours of recording space. They are also small and easy to carry around. With the agreement of others involved, you could record meetings, talks or lectures and make notes from your recordings. But you can also record your notes at the time.

Mini-disk and digital recorders are more expensive than cassette recorders, but are more versatile. You can record and then later feed this into the voice recognition package on your computer. You might find that this is more convenient than lugging a laptop computer around with you.

Portable keyboards
These are robust keyboards (not laptops) with a built-in carrying handle and a reasonable amount of memory. They are light, relatively inexpensive (£200) and have very basic word-processing facilities. You can take them anywhere – they have rechargeable batteries – and, if you have a computer, you can transfer what you have written when you get home.

⌨ High tech – Computers and software
Laptop and palmtop computers
You could use a laptop as your main computer but they are expensive and relatively fragile. They can get damaged and stolen. A palmtop is more restricted in its facilities. It is also very small – a computer that you can hold in your hand. Notes that you make on it can be transferred to an ordinary computer and edited. The keyboard is very small and you may find it awkward. If you need to carry a word processor around – to meetings, lectures or visiting people – then a portable keyboard may be the best option.

Technology to help with numbers

⌨ Medium tech
Most modern telephones can store numbers you use frequently.

There are many calculators on the market including ones that talk (try the RNIB for information, www.rnib.org). Don't buy one that is more complicated than you need.

⌨ High tech – Computers and software
Most computers have a calculator package installed. In addition, they all come with spreadsheets such as Excel which can help with calculations, keeping accounts etc. There are various maths packages available. We recommend going on a course on using spreadsheets at your local college to find out more about these versatile packages.

Technology to help with checking your work

Much of the technology we have mentioned so far is also useful for checking your work. We have summarised this in the table below. Work produced on a word processor is neat and easier to check.

I changed all the settings to make my screen easier to read. This way, I can spot my mistakes easily.

Have I used the correct word?	Reading pen. Text reader. Thesaurus. Dictionary.
Is my grammar correct?	Read onto tape or diskette. Text reader. Grammar checker.
Have I said what I wanted to say?	Read onto tape or diskette. Text reader.
Is the punctuation correct?	Read onto tape or diskette. Text reader.
Have I spelt the word correctly?	Spell checker. Text reader.
General proof-reading	Use the zoom facility to enlarge the print to 150. Mistakes can show up best like this.

Technology to help with organisation

Medium tech
There are various inexpensive ways to help with organisation:

- A pocket-sized electronic organiser has many facilities for storing information, telephone numbers, addresses, dates – and it will remind you of appointments.
- Many mobile phones have similar features.
- Palmtops (as explained above).

High tech – Computers and software
Software packages designed to help you to organise your ideas are sometimes based on mind maps; others draw flow diagrams or allow you to brainstorm, sort and order your ideas. New products are always coming onto the market, so we suggest that you discuss your needs with a specialist. Browse your local computer centre. Some packages have free 'tasters' on the Internet.

More on technology

Printers

If you have a computer or a portable keyboard, you will need a printer. Get the best you can afford – make colour a priority. Throughout this book we have mentioned how useful it is to work in colour. If you are using any of the standard or specialist packages to produce work you will want to print it out in colour. Ink cartridges are expensive, so be economical in your printing:

- Try to get into the habit of reading as much as you can on screen by altering the font, changing the background colour and using the zoom facility to increase the size.
- Print out in draft quality only until you are sure your work is complete and error free.
- Don't print out everything from the Internet – you often get pages you don't want. Either copy and paste into a Word file and then edit, or save the Internet (html) file in a folder on disk.

Software

There is a wealth of software available that will be useful and helpful. Again the advice is don't rush out and buy something. Here are some things you can do first:

- Consider carefully what your needs are and what you really want to do. The activities at the start and end of this chapter give you time to think about this.
- Ask other users what they find helpful – ask them to show you or let you try theirs. Ask them what works and what might be frustrating about the package. Don't try to use or copy their software onto your computer – this is illegal. You won't have access to any help or be able to get updates.
- Look for sample packages to download from the Internet to try out.
- Contact a specialist.
- Don't buy everything at once because it takes time to learn properly about software. Make sure you have enough time to get to grips with it – build your training time into your weekly diary.

The Internet

The Internet will give you access to a vast amount of information, advice, dictionaries, encyclopaedias, reference works and websites of every kind. Many websites are ephemeral – here today and gone tomorrow – or are allowed to fall out of date. You may have no way of assessing their quality, but don't be put off – use the Internet intelligently, just as you would a library. If you find a site that you would like to return to, add it to your Favourites (if you use Microsoft's Internet Explorer) or Bookmarks (if you use Netscape Navigator). We have listed some of our favourite sites on the CD-ROM. The *Rough Guide to the Internet* (available in all major bookshops) is a very useful pocket-sized book that is frequently updated. We recommend you to buy a copy if you are relatively new to the Internet.

Another advantage of using the Internet is **email**. This flexible and informal method of communication has many advantages.

What might *you* need?

✍ ACTIVITY 21 – What do I need?

Now look back at your answers to Activity 20 and answer the remaining questions on the sheet – also given below:

If you already have some medium or high tech items, how can you use them in ways you hadn't thought of before? Note three things that you will try soon.

What ideas have you found for the three dyslexic difficulties you have suggested need a technical remedy?

Justifying the expense
If you find something that is useful but costly, think whether it could be useful in other ways. For example, would other members of your family find it useful? Would it be useful at work? Your employer may be prepared to purchase some software for you. Some software licences will allow you to load it onto more than one machine – your home computer, for example.

Training
Ensure that you get good training to get you started. For more high-tech items such as computers and software, some follow-up training would be useful. You can't learn everything at once. Try your local college for courses or evening classes.

There is a lot of technology lying around not being used – you may have some yourself. The advice in this chapter may have persuaded you to use it at last. Don't be tempted to rush out and buy – seek good advice from a specialist supplier (see appendix c). Talk to others about what they have found useful.

If you buy expensive equipment, don't forget to check whether you have insurance that covers you for loss or damage, including if you take it away from home.

Technology has made both my life and work so much easier. It's been worth the extra bit it cost me.

In this chapter we've described lots of technology that's available currently. Keep a look out for anything new.

Finally, here is a list of low tech items we said you might find useful.

🗁 LOW TECH ITEMS

We suggest that you keep a supply of the following. Local office suppliers and shops such as Woolworths usually stock low-priced items.

A4 pad of squared paper for keeping writing neat, for doing calculations or for planning.

A3 or larger plain pads – such as flipchart pads, wallpaper lining paper for posters and planning.

Highlighter pens and felt-tips in a range of colours.

Envelope files in a range of colours.

Plastic document wallets in a range of colours for filing or for makeshift coloured overlays.

Document boxes for filing the wallets.

Pens and pencils of all shapes, sizes and colours – fat, thin, fibre-tipped etc. Marker pens for posters.

Post-it Notes™ or similar semi-sticky notes in a range of shapes and colours for brainstorming, memos, etc.

Coloured page markers (semi-adhesive).

Index cards for personal dictionary, facts to learn etc.

Small address book for personal dictionary.

Coloured file dividers.

Sticky labels in a range of shapes and colours – good for labelling.

Scrapbooks.

Pack of A4 paper in the tint you find easier to read.

Tinted card for making bookmarks and tracking rulers.

Selection of coloured paperclips.

Save scrap paper for practising writing, testing spelling, making spider diagrams, printing out drafts etc.

Copy holder – cookery-book holder.

CRAVEN COLLEGE

10
Looking wider

Why, then the world's mine oyster
(from *The Merry Wives of Windsor* (Act 2, scene 2) by William Shakespeare)

This chapter looks at the wider aspects of dyslexia – we look at the attitudes of others generally and family, friends and colleagues in particular. We look at how other professionals and organisations can help. We suggest ways of coping in education, whether it is for leisure, training at work, further or higher education. Finally we look at help in the workplace. The epilogue encourages you to think about where you go from here.

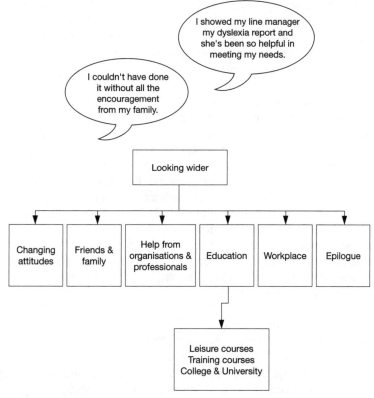

Figure 19 Looking wider

Changing attitudes to dyslexia

'Word blindness'

In the 19th century, as education became more common, some people found they had unexpected difficulty with reading. This difficulty was put down to 'word blindness', a term which persisted until well into the 20th century. Only a very few people were offered help – others drifted into the more practical trades and professions at which they often excelled.

'It must be your fault'

When individuals could not learn to read or write for no obvious reason, all too often they were seen as being to blame. They were called slow, thick, lazy or uneducable – some educators even claimed that they came from a 'bad' background! Some people might have been lucky enough to have been taught by an inspired teacher using a multisensory approach. Such a teacher recognised their method was successful, although they did not necessarily know why.

'Damaged centres in the brain'

In the early 20th century, scientists studying the brain realised that the things we do seem to relate to specific centres of the brain. This was a rather simplified approach but it laid the foundations for modern neurology. People researching dyslexia suggested that it was due to damage to some of these centres.

'Some brains don't work the same way'

It wasn't until doctors started to investigate spoken and written language deficits in stroke patients that the first neurological research into dyslexia was carried out. This showed damage in the left hemisphere of the brain which was later to be identified as a main control area for language. This kind of dyslexia is called 'acquired' dyslexia. By examining brains, further research revealed the different ways brains used and handled data (see chapter 2). At the same time, the pioneering work of Samuel Orton in the US suggested that dyslexia was due to abnormal development in children and coined the term 'developmental dyslexia' to cover the more common occurrence. Orton believed that remediation was entirely possible so some enlightened schools and teachers began using remediation programmes.

'Some brains work differently'

Further understanding of the brain using the relatively recent and expensive brain-scanning equipment has led to the neurological differences being established beyond all doubt. In the UK, direct phonics teaching was introduced with the National Literacy Strategy.

In the 21st century

Dyslexia is now well recognised and accepted throughout the world, but there are still many people whose understanding is not up to date. So be prepared to come up against people who:

- have outdated attitudes;
- think it is just to do with reading and spelling;
- may not spot your dyslexia and see it as carelessness, stupidity or laziness.

Many teachers know a bit about dyslexia but may be unsure how best to help. There are good reasons for this:

- Teacher training does not spend enough time on teaching reading – and even less time on dyslexia.
- Resources are always stretched.
- Teachers can learn more about dyslexia on postgraduate courses but these are expensive and time-consuming.

Many other people know nothing really except from the odd headline or article in a newspaper, from TV or radio programmes. They may still hold old prejudices – 'people who can't read must be stupid or lazy' etc. They may not be aware of further difficulties beyond reading, writing and spelling such as memory, organisational and other difficulties. Attitudes are improving but perhaps not as quickly as they should be – and certainly not as fast as the science.

You may have to work alongside some of these attitudes.

Friends and family

The attitudes of, and support from, the people around you are vital to your success. Above all, they should be encouraging and positive – they should see you not as dyslexic, but as a person with skills, abilities and needs.

✍ ACTIVITY 22

Take a moment to think of something that someone has said or done for you that has made you feel good or given you the incentive to try something new.

Who was it?	What did they say or do?

My colleague was very impressed with my creative solutions – she took on the task of writing them up for use.

It helps if those around you understand what dyslexia is, and what your particular dyslexia means for you. But it isn't absolutely necessary. People can simply celebrate difference and understand that we all need to do some things differently from others. This is what makes the world such an interesting place.

Support from those close to you
There are many things that those around you can do to help and we have listed some below. You can highlight the things you would like people to do – and perhaps put their names by particular items. There's space to add your own ideas too.

Positive attitudes:		Who?
Be accepting of your quirks	Give them chapter 3 to read	
Get an understanding of what dyslexia is	Give them chapter 2 to read	
For them to ask you what they can do to help ...	... rather than making assumptions about what would be useful for you	

Give you loads of encouragement to keep you going	Praise and encouragement raises the spirits	
Concentrate on your strengths ...	... and overlook your weaknesses	

Practical help:		
Help your reading fluency through paired reading	See chapter 4	
Let you use their computer or help you with yours	See chapter 9	
Help with checking your work	See CD-ROM Writing section ⊘ for positive ways to do this	
Rewriting or rewording instructions.	Often instructions are poor translations from another language	
Reminders	Giving gentle reminders of things that need to be done	
Help with costs of assessment, equipment, books, tutoring etc.	Tokens or cheques for birthdays and other celebrations	

Help with checking your work
Detailed guidance is given on the CD-ROM. The message is clear – it helps you to learn if you make your own corrections. So ask your checker to simply indicate that there is an error but allow you to try to spot it.

For example:

> The <u>tranquility</u> and beauty of this huge park is <u>rivaled</u> only by its
> variety of animal life – a <u>kalidoscope</u> of diving sea lions, talking
> mynahs, chortling <u>chimpanzies</u> and stately king penguins.

The checker has underlined the misspelled words but not corrected
them. It is up to the writer to correct them. The correct spellings are:
tranquillity, rivalled, kaleidoscope, chimpanzees.

Supporting others
You're unlikely to be the only dyslexic person you know of. One in 10
people have some dyslexic difficulties – for one in five of those the
difficulties can be quite problematical. In a large family there may be
several members affected in some way because dyslexia has a genetic
basis. If you work with 50 people, you can expect to find about five with
similar difficulties. You can help them because you have some
understanding of their feelings and frustrations.

Look out for local support groups – they will include parents, dyslexic
young people and adults. Your local library will have details. Often there
are regular meetings with speakers on a range of subjects. As we write,
a local group programme includes the following: 'Educational games',
'Self-esteem, stress and dyslexia'. We strongly encourage you to seek
out your local group. You will find people who understand, who are non-
judgemental – a safe environment to share your problems and try things
out. And you can help them too. Groups often have an advice line run by
volunteers. Your expertise will be invaluable.

If you have dyslexic children or know of some, then reading to and with
them is symbiotic – you both gain. We looked at this in chapter 4.

Help from organisations and professionals

Counselling, professional help etc.
Counsellors can help people make sense of their painful experiences
and understand them better. They can work with a client on their issues
such as low self-esteem and depression which can result from 'not
being listened to' for a long time.

The strain of being constantly misinterpreted is enormous. Most children
develop low self-esteem if they are regularly criticised – they are
effectively being told that they are no good (therefore unlovable)
whenever they do something the adult doesn't like. Low self-esteem

may lead to depression or frustration expressed as anti-social behaviour. Some people may find these frustrations have led to serious problems.

Someone who is dyslexic also has to cope with the fact that they don't know why it is happening to them. They tend to blame themselves when they lose things or turn up late etc., unaware of the role dyslexia may be playing in this. It will help if a counsellor knows about dyslexia – if you decide to see someone, tell them. If you are not sure whether you are dyslexic, then explaining the difficulties you have in reading, organising or remembering will help them to work with your feelings about these issues.

It can be enormously helpful to share your feelings about everything that has happened with someone who is independent and who won't judge you. A counsellor's role is to help you to cope more effectively. They can also help you to handle stress.

Optometrists

In chapter 4 we mentioned how useful coloured transparent overlays can be with reading – they seem to hold the print on the page and help to make reading more comfortable. There are sound scientific reasons for this. A large proportion of dyslexic people have problems with visual discomfort (as do a few non-dyslexics). If you have tried coloured overlays (or even makeshift ones using coloured transparent folders) and found an improvement in comfort with reading, then we strongly recommend that you consult an optometrist to talk about tinted lenses.

In fact, we recommend that you see an optometrist if you experience any discomfort: distortion, blurring, headaches, difficulty concentrating when reading. The cause may be to do with the eye and this should be corrected first. If some symptoms still persist, then you can see an optometrist who specialises in dyslexia and the use of a piece of equipment called the intuitive colorimeter. You local optician may have such a person on their staff but, if not, they should be able to tell you how to contact one.

Education

Education providers are often very helpful in offering facilities to meet needs. They are required by law to make reasonable adjustments for disabled people under part 4 of the Disability Discrimination Act 1995. Dyslexia is defined as a disability under this Act. It may, therefore, be a good idea to mention your dyslexia to the college.

The driving test

It's possible to be given extra time to complete the theory part of the test. You will need proof of your dyslexia for this allowance. If you have difficulty distinguishing your left from your right, it is also acceptable during the practical test to ask the examiner to point out the direction to take.

Leisure courses

Like many, you may be concerned about signing up for evening or day classes. You are making quite a financial commitment and you may be concerned about what you could be asked to do. Here are some points to consider:

- Choose a course that really interests you.
- Talk to the course organiser beforehand or at the end of the first session. Explain that you will be able to get so much more out of the course if they can introduce the plan for each session first. This gives you an idea of what to expect.
- Take a friend who will be happy to go over anything you are not sure of afterwards.
- Go to a 'taster' session if it is offered.

Languages for leisure

If you have had difficulties learning your own language, this may put you off from attempting another. But it wasn't learning to *speak* your own language that gave you the problem. So build up your confidence with another language by concentrating on conversation classes at first. You may find that you are really good at speaking but that it's hard to learn the words. It can be difficult to learn a word that you can't see or you don't know how to spell. Chapter 8 offers ideas for learning that you can develop. All language learners agree that if you don't use it, you lose it – so practise as often as you can.

- There are many good language computer packages available that use multisensory learning – hearing and seeing at the same time.
- Find a native speaker who will speak slowly for you. They are often eager to help and you may be able to help them with their spoken English too.

It goes without saying that anyone who has difficulties learning their first language will find it difficult to learn another; all the same problems will arise. Dyslexics can often learn to *speak* another language well by 'immersion' – living in a foreign country for example. But reading and writing is likely to be very problematical.

You are likely to find Italian or Spanish easier than French. French is similar to English in its non-transparency (see chapter 2). Look at all the words with silent endings for example. German falls somewhere in the middle. Pronunciation of groups of letters may be complex but, once you've grasped this, it tends always to be the same.

This *doesn't* mean that you shouldn't attempt foreign languages. Getting a feel for speaking the language first will help. After all, this is the way you learnt your first language and there *are* dyslexic French, Italian and Chinese people! It is a worldwide phenomenon.

Actually, I seem to have a really good French accent but I don't know how to spell the words!

Music
Do you have a good ear for a tune?
Do you have a good sense of rhythm?
Do you want to read music?

Dyslexia can be an asset in music – the 'right-brained' creative and holistic skills are useful. But some things can give rise to difficulties so here are just a few ideas to help:

- As with other things, make music multisensory: yes, hear it, but also feel it and see it too.
- Practise playing an instrument with your eyes shut to help you to feel where the notes are.
- Use colour to help you remember the notes on the lines and spaces of the music.
- Apply chunking – learn the notes of music first, then apply the rhythm.
- Keep going when playing. Ignore your mistakes. Record what you are doing and then go back, pick out any mistakes and try to identify what caused you to make the mistake.
- Try playing (or singing) the difficult bit really slowly until you get it mostly right – then increase the speed until you get it all right.
- Look for patterns in music. Learn these and then identify variations.
- Listen to a recording of the piece over and again until it becomes familiar.
- Memorise it using whatever strategies you can devise. Knowing the music well can liberate expression.
- A useful website with helpful ideas is www.musicgoals.com/index.htm

Sight reading can be very difficult if you are dyslexic. Look in the Memory section of the CD-ROM for an idea that has worked for some people.

Going on training courses
What are the possible issues?

- Having to present something in a group.
- Having to read something quickly.
- Having to write something.

You can:

- Ask for reading material in advance.
- Volunteer to lead a discussion and then reasonably ask someone else to act as note-taker.
- Offer to write a report giving yourself a reasonable timescale but ask for a copy of the PowerPoint presentation or relevant notes to help you.
- Explain calmly that you work better by speaking and listening, so you would like agreement to tape record discussions.
- Ask them to briefly summarise what they are going to do, e.g. 'Could you please take us through the programme first?'
- Ask them to sum up if necessary.

College and university
If you are thinking of going to college or university it is important to choose your course carefully. Dyslexia presents an additional dimension to your learning – coping in an environment in which most people are not dyslexic. You will not be able to avoid doing some things but you should be able to do most of them, though differently.

Choosing a course
You need to consider a number of points to help you choose your course. You'll have to balance the advantages of some against the disadvantages of others. To help you do this, mark each of the points on the list below in order of importance. Try grading each as either 'extremely', 'very', or 'not very' important. Don't put everything into one column – force yourself to prioritise.

	Extremely	Very	Not very
How important is your interest in the subject or topic?			
How important are the implications for your career?			
How important is previous experience or knowledge of the topic?			
How important is advice from others?			
How important is relevant work experience?			
How important is being aware of demands that are likely to be very difficult for you?			
How important is it that there should be other ways of meeting those demands?			
How important is finding out about other courses that might be more suitable for your needs?			
How important is an academic qualification to you?			

You should now have a good idea of what is important for you in choosing a course.

Strategies for coping at college or university
Most colleges and universities offer a confidential student support service which will help you:

- get a dyslexia assessment or reassessment;
- apply for additional time in examinations or assignments;
- apply, if appropriate, for the disabled student allowance (DSA) which can supply both teaching support and computer technology/software.
- a mentor.

University libraries are also getting much better at offering guidance in using their books and resources. There is an excellent book called *Dyslexia at College* (see appendix B).

Area of possible difficulty	Strategy for coping at college or university
Administrative requirements Signing up for courses, exams, field trips Knowing who to go to for what	Lists & flow charts Card index Personal mentor
Organising studies Planning Knowing when and where something happens Knowing where rooms are Meeting deadlines	Wallcharts & timetables Coloured labels & files Diaries Electronic organiser Negotiate for quiet workspace
Volume & pressure of work Prioritising Getting help	New list at the start of each day Card index of places to go for help Eating properly and getting exercise Chunking, taking breaks
Study skills and concentration Coping with reading, experiments and surveys, field or lab work Reading instructions Writing reports Coping with background noise Interruptions	Colour coding filing trays & boxes Highlighting Using space creatively Using mind maps & spider diagrams Using templates Using the Student Support Service *Dyslexia at College* – see appendix B.
Time Knowing how long it takes to do something Getting to the right place at the right time Getting the right book at the right time	Digital watch Mobile phone facilities Electronic reminders on computer Tell someone exactly how long it took you

Independent living Organising your food, your money, your washing	Chapter 6
Attitudes Coping with lecturers & tutors who are not meeting your needs	Useful phrases to engage understanding Address issues of harassment

Many students with dyslexia study successfully in further and higher education – you can too. Adults can also study part-time at many institutions and through the Open University.

Don't put everything down to dyslexia. Talk to the tutor and the other students – it may be that everyone is finding it difficult!

Workplace issues

Don't skip this section if you are not 'employed'. Working at home, looking after children or parents, doing voluntary work or working at being retired – all involve responsibilities, planning, organisation and so on. There's something here for you.

✍ ACTIVITY 23

Think about the things that concern you at work. At work:

- You worry that someone may 'find out' and think less of you.
- You may choose work that doesn't involve too much writing.
- You may get more easily stressed by deadlines for reports.
- You worry about writing/spelling.
- You are easily distracted by noise and activity.

Which of these are you concerned about? What don't you like doing and what do you try to avoid?

Now think about a few things that you are good at in your job, that you enjoy doing, that you feel confident to do:

- Meeting and talking to other people.
- Solving problems.

- Finding new and better ways of doing things.
- Giving informal presentations.
- Good with computer software.

It's not all bad. The trick in work (and life) is to **emphasise** the things you are good at and use these strengths to help you with the things that give you problems. So use this book and the people close to you to help you identify these strengths.

In chapters 4 to 9 we introduced lots of ideas and strategies that we know work for dyslexic adults. You can adapt these for use in your work depending on your tasks and responsibilities. We hope you'll try them ... if you haven't already.

Dyslexia can give rise to problems at work in seven broad areas:

- Procedures – the order in which things should be done.
- Organisation – planning.
- Workload – coping with tasks in a given time.
- Literacy – filing, reading, writing, spelling.
- Time – how long things take and when.
- Concentration – coping with noise and interruptions.
- Attitudes of others.

We have listed some common tasks under each heading in the activity below and suggested some strategies you can use.

✍ ACTIVITY 24

Look at each of the seven headings. Highlight any tasks which you have to do in your job. Add any that are specific to your job and are not on the list. Think about some strategies you could use. Put a circle round those you'd like to try ... and try them.

Tasks	Strategies (chapter number in brackets)
Procedures Remembering the order you have to do things in Remembering who has responsibility for what	Lists & flow charts (5)

Organisation Planning Knowing when and where something happens Knowing where things are	Wallcharts & timetables (6) Coloured labels & files (6) Trade tasks with others Mind maps (5)
Workload Prioritising Delegating	New list at the start of each day (6)
Literacy issues Filing Reading instructions Writing & reading reports	Colour coding filing trays & boxes Highlighting Using space creatively Using mind maps & spider diagrams Using templates Using a secretary/PA (Chapters 4–6)
Time Knowing how long it takes to do something Getting to the right place at the right time	Digital watch (6) Mobile phone facility
Concentration Coping with background noise, interruptions	Negotiate for a quiet work area (6)
Attitudes Coping with colleagues who are not understanding Being called untidy, careless, stupid	Useful phrases to engage understanding (see below) Address issues of harassment

Should you tell work colleagues about your dyslexia?
- Dyslexia is becoming better understood but there are still many misconceptions about the subject, so you need to make a judgement about whom to tell.
- You can just make your **needs** known. Dyslexia is a label and labels can be misleading. Dyslexia is idiosyncratic – each person has a different set of strengths and difficulties just like everyone else. No two people experience dyslexia in the same way – just as no two Marys are the same!

Words and phrases to help you

Most of us find it hard to say how we would like to be treated. We may not be able to find the right words in a given situation. It helps to have some phrases ready. You could keep them handy in a notebook. Practise saying them until you feel comfortable with them and can summon them up easily.

Try using or adapting these:

☺ It may not look like it but my workspace is organised the way I work best.

☺ I work better when I talk it through and someone else makes notes.

☺ My spelling is variable – is correct spelling important for this?

☺ I need some time to get my head around this.

☺ It really helps when you explain what you are going to do first.

☺ Please can you send me everything electronically so I can reformat if I need to?

☺ Can you write that down for me? Just a moment while I write that down.

☺ Are those instructions written down anywhere? I would find that really useful.

☺ Can I have a photocopy of that?

☺ That's useful – please will you send that on an e-mail to me?

☺ Your encouragement makes a lot of difference. Tell me when you think it's good.

If you have a dyslexic employee, then you can use all the ideas suggested above. Talk the job through with them so that together you can identify the appropriate support and strategies to use.

Epilogue: where do you go from here?

Wherever you want to go!!

There is such a lot that you can do to achieve your aims. We hope you have already discovered some new ideas in this book. If you don't feel confident about something, you should by now realise that there are many ways you can maximise your potential:

- Decide what it is you want to do.
- Then identify the strategies that are going to get you there.

Over the years you may have been given inappropriate or very little help to overcome your difficulties. Don't give yourself a hard time because you may have been given the wrong tools for **you** in learning how to learn. The very fact that you are reading this book is testimony to your persistence and determination which are two of the most important characteristics of successful learning. Add to that the way you think as a dyslexic adult – usually creatively and holistically. These are talents that can give you a head start in new ways of looking at yourself and the world.

We weren't expecting you to read this book, from cover to cover. You may have dipped into it over a period of days, months, even years. You may have come straight to this page to see how it all ends! Now you are here ...

Pause

Since starting to read this book:

What have you tried?
What has been a useful learning experience?
What might you do next?

When we finished writing this book we reflected on all the dyslexic adults we have met over the past 20 odd years. We thought about some of their qualities that seemed to stand out, the positive aspects of dyslexia that we have mentioned throughout this book. These are the adjectives that come to mind:

Determined
Creative
Persistent
Quirky
Expressive
Inventive
Empathetic
Insightful
Amazing

and having a sense of humour and strong sense of achievement.

So we dedicate this book to all those we've known who have inspired us to write it.

Appendix A
Checklist for dyslexia

If you think you might be dyslexic, this checklist is for you to work through. It includes a range of questions that help identify dyslexia-type difficulties.

Think carefully, but not for too long, about your answers. You might find it useful to ask other people who know you well to comment or help you complete the form.

 Please tick the appropriate boxes and add any comments that come to mind as you reflect on each section. There Is a printable version on the CD-ROM.

When you are writing, do you . . .	Yes	No	Sometimes
Find organising ideas on paper more difficult than explaining them verbally?			
Find it hard to listen and take notes at the same time?			
Find it hard to copy things accurately?			
Struggle to remember the word you want to describe or name something?			
Miss out letters or parts (syllables) of words?			
Confuse or reverse letters in a word (e.g. b/d, f/t, n/v)?			
Anything else about your writing such as the style – is it tidy?			

When you are reading, do you often ...	Yes	No	Sometimes
Misread or misinterpret a passage?			
Find reading an arduous and slow process?			
Only make sense of a passage by rereading it several times?			
Take a long time to scan a passage for the main point?			
Anything else about your reading such as coping with reading new and unfamiliar words?			

Thinking back over your early years, do you remember ...	Yes	No	Sometimes
Being later in learning to read or write than others?			
Not wanting to read aloud in class?			
Finding it hard to memorise spellings?			
Misreading numbers or writing them incorrectly?			
Having difficulty learning multiplication tables?			
Anything else you remember: e.g. clumsiness, lack of coordination in ball games, difficulty with organisation?			

In your everyday life now, do you find yourself generally ...	Yes	No	Sometimes
Avoiding reading?			
Avoiding writing?			
Having difficulty when filling in forms?			
Tending to get telephone numbers mixed up?			

Confusing dates and missing appointments?			
Not being able to find the right word for something?			
Needing written reminders for everything and still forgetting?			
Having difficulty organising your paperwork?			
Confusing left and right?			
Dreading being given verbal instructions?			
Are your difficulties shared by other family members?			

If you ticked 'Yes' or 'Sometimes' to most of the questions in one or more of the sections, you may be dyslexic.

You are likely to find many of the ideas and strategies in this book useful.

There are a number of helplines, both local and national, available for you to discuss dyslexia with someone. You can start by contacting the useful addresses in appendix c.

If you have ticked 'No' more often than 'Yes'.

Many people experience some of these difficulties, especially when they are under pressure. They may arise from many different sources such as previous school experiences, hearing problems or a change in language. You may not be dyslexic or you may be mildly dyslexic. But you may still find some ideas in this book useful.

Appendix B
Useful and interesting books

General interest for dyslexic adults

Every Letter Counts – Winning in Life Despite Dyslexia by Susan Hampshire (Corgi, 1991).
Several useful descriptions of dyslexic adults and some advice on strategies.

In the Mind's Eye by Thomas G. West (Prometheus, 1997).
An exploration of the creative side of dyslexia.

How to Mind Map by Tony Buzan (HarperCollins, 2002).
A good guide to making mind maps.

The Speed Reading Book by Tony Buzan (BBC Consumer Publishing, 2003).

Handwriting

Teach Yourself Better Handwriting by Rosemary Sassoon (Hodder Arnold Teach Yourself, 2003).
A practical guide to handwriting problems and strategies.

Spelling

The Ace Spelling Dictionary by David Moseley and Catherine Nical (LDA, 1991).

This dictionary is arranged on sounds rather than actual spellings. You identify the first sound of the word and follow the clear instructions.

Hamlyn's Good Spelling Dictionary (Hamlyn, 1979).
Good – gives all parts of a word, e.g. give, giving, gave.

The Pergamon Dictionary of Perfect Spelling edited by Christine Maxwell (Arnold-Wheaton, 1979).

Grammar

Basic Grammar by Don Shiach (John Murray, 1995).

Rediscover Grammar by David Crystal (Longman, 1997).
A really entertaining book that starts from scratch.

Punctuation

Basic Punctuation by Don Shiach (John Murray (Pub) Ltd., 1995).

The Internet

Rough Guide to the Internet
Good, basic guide written in plain English.

Books for students

Dyslexia at College by T.R. Miles and D.E. Gilroy (Routledge, 1995).
Really sound advice for anyone thinking of going to college. Don't try to read it all in one go.

The Study Skills Handbook by Stella Cottrell (Palgrave, 2003).
An excellent book for all students in higher education. Well presented and includes lots of ideas for tackling a range of difficulties and improving study skills.

Theoretical aspects

Dyslexia: Theory and Good Practice edited by Angela Fawcett (Whurr, 2001).

Mapping the Mind by Rita Carter (Phoenix, 2000).
Covers more about the workings of the brain generally.

Appendix C
Useful addresses

Adult Dyslexia Organisation
336 Brixton Road
London
SW9 7AA

Helpline 020 7924 9559

A helpful, professional and friendly organisation for adults who have dyslexia, and for professionals and others with an interest in adults. Publishes newsletters, fact sheets, guidance notes and so on, and runs meetings and conferences. Quickest route to their website is probably through the BDA website.

British Dyslexia Association
98 London Road
Reading
Berks
RG1 5AU

Helpline 01189 668 271

www.bda-dyslexia.org.uk/

Has some useful fact sheets for adults. Many local branches, some of which have adult groups. Useful for assessments and learning skills support. A lot of information is available from the website.

Dyslexia Institute
133 Gresham Road
Staines
Middlesex
TW18 2AJ

Tel. 01784 222 300

Offers tuition and assessments for all ages throughout the UK.

There are many local organisations also offering tuition and assessment. Look in your local library or phone book for details.

iANSYST
Fen House
Fen Road
Cambridge
CB4 1UN

Tel. 01223 42 01 01

E-mail sales@dyslexic.com

National and international experts in equipment and software for dyslexics. Very helpful organisation that can help you to decide on the best computer packages for you.

International Dyslexia Association (USA and affiliated countries)
Chester Building, Suite 382
8600 LaSalle Road
Baltimore,
Maryland 21286-2044
USA

Telephone: (001) 410-296-0232

A non-profit, scientific, and educational organisation dedicated to the study and treatment of the learning disability, dyslexia.

Australia and New Zealand

Specific Learning Disabilities Federation (SPELD) is a non-profit organisation that provides advice and services to children and adults with specific learning difficulties, such as dyslexia. It has member associations throughout Australia and New Zealand:

SPELD
298 Portrush Road,
Kensington,
South Australia, 5068

SPELD NZ
c/o Secretary,
PO Box 25,
Dargaville

Appendix D
Glossary

Most of these words are explained where they occur in the main text. Some are on the CD-ROM only.

Accommodations Allowances made in examinations such as extra time. Sometimes called 'concessions'.

Alliteration A string of words beginning with the same <u>sound</u> such as *Sing a song of sixpence ...*

Alphabetic strategy According to Frith, the second stage of learning to read – by sounding out the letters.

Assessment An interview and a series of tests designed to identify dyslexia and your strengths.

Asymmetric Something that isn't symmetric.

Auditory To do with hearing.

Automaticity The ability to do things automatically.

Blend Two or more consonant sounds that run together such as *br, pl, rt.*

Cerebellum The section at the lower back of the brain which is responsible for things we do automatically. Often referred to as the brain's 'auto-pilot'.

Chromosome Strings of genes found in all living cells.

Chunking What smart dyslexics do – break things down into manageable amounts.

Coding Transferring word sounds into letters and words.

Cognitive ability A measure of learning skills such as memory, phonological awareness and fluency.

Cognitive learning style How you think and approach your learning.

Coloured overlays *See* Mears-Irlen overlays.

Compensated dyslexic A dyslexic person whose literacy and numeracy attainment is reasonable because of good strategies. They may still have considerable difficulties.

Comprehension	What you understand about a piece of text you have read.
Concessions	Allowances made in examinations such as extra time. More usually called *accommodations* these days.
Concrete example	An example that you can readily identify with; explains a concept.
Consonant	21 of the 26 letters of the alphabet – those that are not vowels (a,e,i,o,u).
Cuisenaire rods	Small coloured sticks that have a different colour for each length. Used for getting the feel of quantity.
Decoding	Taking the letters or groups of letters and translating into sounds to make words.
Denominator	In maths, the bottom number of a fraction: e.g. in 1/2 the 2 is the denominator.
Diagnosis	In dyslexia a diagnosis is made on the basis of cognitive skills being less well developed.
Dyscalculia	A difficulty with maths that is unexpected. Some people with dyslexia are affected.
Dyslexia	A specific learning difficulty.
Dyslexia learning style	Dyslexics tend to think holistically, intuitively and are creative.
Electronic dictionary	Available as pocket-sized objects – you can look up the meaning or spelling of a word without using a book.
Fluency	The ability of the brain to do or think something over and over and more and more quickly without being conscious of it.
Font	The style of letters used in print.
Frontal lobe	The front part of the brain that deals with thinking, planning and conceptualisation.
General intellectual ability	A measure of ability made by combining the results of verbal and non-verbal reasoning tests.
Genes (genetics)	Parts of a chromosome that carry the code for development of living things (the study of genes).

Gypsy method	A method of multiplying using the fingers of both hands. It is particularly useful for 6–10 times. tables.
Hemisphere	One half of a sphere. One half of the brain.
Holistic	Taking an overall approach. Seeing things as a whole.
Human genome	The total genetic make up of a human being.
Intuitive colorimeter	An instrument used by an optometrist to find the best colour light to help prevent print blurring or distorting.
Literacy	Ability to read and write.
Logographic strategy	According to Frith, the first stage of learning to read – by recognising the look of a word.
Magnocells	Cells in the brain responsible for processing information.
Mears-Irlen overlays	Coloured sheets of plastic that can help to stabilise print and make it more comfortable to read.
Metacognition	Understanding the way you learn.
Mnemonic	A trick for remembering things. Pronounced 'nem-onic', the m is silent.
Motor skills	Skills that involve movement such as catching a ball.
Multisensory learning	Employing more than one sense when you learn – it helps to learn things using many senses.
Needs assessment	An opportunity to be tested by an expert to see what your needs are and what solutions might be useful.
Neurological	To do with the body's nervous system, especially the brain.
Neurons	The cells in the brain responsible for its activity.
Neuroscience	The study of how the brain functions.
Non-transparent language	A language like English where there is little correspondence between speech sounds and letters do not correspond regularly.

Onset and rime The onset is the first sound of a word or syllable. The rime is the second sound.

Optometrist A professional practitioner qualified to examine eyes and prescribe treatment such as spectacles, contact lenses etc. Often referred to as opticians.

Orthographic strategy According to Frith, the third stage of learning to read – recognising chunks of words and relating them to sounds.

Paired reading A strategy of reading alternately with a good reader helps to improve fluency and confidence.

Percentile The result of a test or tests quoted as the level you have reached being higher than that percentage of people.

Phoneme A single speech unit: sh-ee-p has three phonemes.

Phonological Relating to language sounds.

Phonology The study of sounds that are found in language. This means the sounds used when you speak rather than sounds made when you scream, laugh or cough.

Post mortem Studies on bodies after death.

Psychometric tests Tests which measure all aspects of mental ability: personality, intelligence, aptitude etc.

Readability level An easily calculated measure of the degree of difficulty of a passage of text.

Reading age An indication of a child's reading skills. It can be above, the same as or below their actual age.

Read-out facility Text to speech packages for the computer – see chapter 9.

Right brained Over-generalised description for the creative skills.

Scanning, scanners A non-invasive method of observing what is happening in internal organs such as the brain. Also, equipment that reads text into a computer.

Scotopic sensitivity A misnomer for visual discomfort not caused by an eye defect.

Screening

Short tests and/or an interview with a specialist to see if you have dyslexic traits, before going for a full assessment.

Sensory learning style

The sense(s) you use most when you learn.

Sequencing

Putting things in a specific order, e.g. alphabetical order.

Spoonerism

Swapping over the first sounds in two words. For example, saying 'par cark' for 'car park'.

Standard score

Test results that have been recalculated so that they can be compared to the performance of a particular group and also across a range of different tests.

Syllable

Part of a word said with one single effort of the voice. So 'sheep' has only one syllable (compare this with a 'phoneme' as described above).

Symmetric

An object where each side of the middle line is a mirror image.

Tracking

How the eye follows a line of print across a page.

Transparent language

A language where the letters or groups of letters always represent the same sound, e.g. Italian.

Visual

To do with seeing.

Visual loop

A model for the brain processing visual information.

Vowel

The letters of the alphabet that are not consonants: a, e, i, o, u – sometimes y.

Index